Helen Mar Johnson, John Muir Orrock

Canadian wild Flowers

Selections from the Writings of Miss Helen M. Johnson with a Sketch of her Life

Helen Mar Johnson, John Muir Orrock

Canadian wild Flowers
Selections from the Writings of Miss Helen M. Johnson with a Sketch of her Life

ISBN/EAN: 9783337111731

Printed in Europe, USA, Canada, Australia, Japan

Cover: Foto ©ninafisch / pixelio.de

More available books at **www.hansebooks.com**

Canadian Wild Flowers:

SELECTIONS FROM THE WRITINGS

OF

MISS HELEN M. JOHNSON,
OF MAGOG, P. Q., CANADA,

WITH

A SKETCH OF HER LIFE.

BY REV. J. M. ORROCK,
EDITOR OF "MESSIAH'S HERALD," BOSTON, MASS.

Good thoughts spring from the human mind
Like flowers from out the ground;
Attractive, fragrant, beautiful,—
To make our joys abound.

BOSTON:
PUBLISHED BY J. M. ORROCK,
74 KNEELAND STREET.
1884.

Preface.

An observance of the hand of God in his providences, as well as of his Spirit in the written Word and in the human heart, has led to the publication of this book. Though more than twenty years have passed since Miss JOHNSON died, her name is like "an ointment poured forth." Many who never knew her personally seem to know her well from her poetic writings : for "as fragrance to the sense of smell, music to the ear, or beauty to the eye, so is poetry to the sensibilities of the heart,—it ministers to a want of our intellectual nature ; this is the secret of its power and the pledge of its perpetuity." A 16mo volume of her " Poems " was published in Boston, in 1855, but has long been out of print. In 1864 the Rev. E. H. Dewart published in Montreal a work entitled " Selections from Canadian Poets," in which ten of her poems were inserted and a very appreciative notice of her given. She also wrote for several papers, so that in various ways her thoughts have been widely disseminated. A desire has often been expressed to have them collected into one volume; but to have all thus republished would not be best. I have therefore attempted only what the title indicates—to make *selections from her writings;* and conclude to send them forth under a name which she herself chose at a time when she had thoughts of getting out a book. Let critics remember that they claim to be only " *Canadian wild flowers*"; yet we feel sure that some of them, for beauty of form and fragrance of truth, will not unfavorably compare with some of the cultivated productions of our classic poets. Miss JOHNSON was better known by her poetry than by her prose writings, yet in the latter are found so many grand thoughts that I have copied from them freely. The biographical sketch, it is hoped, will add interest to the book, especially as so many of her diary notes have been interwoven. Some of her pieces are here printed for the first time. The prize poem on "The Surrender of Quebec" is given in full. In the Preface to her "Poems" she said: "I have been cheered and encouraged by the thought that perhaps through my instrumentality the heart of some humble believer might be comforted, and some wretched wanderer, weary of the vanities of earth, be directed to the only source of life and happiness. Should such be the case, the brightest hopes of the authoress will be fulfilled, and she herself be amply compensated for her care and labor." With a sincere desire to aid in the direction thus indicated this little work is now sent forth.

J. M. O.

Brookline, Mass.,
  June 22, 1884.

CONTENTS.

PAGE.

LIFE-SKETCH:

   Birth-place—The Forest (a poem)—Conviction of sin—Baptism and Resolutions—Experience—Diary notes in verse—Sufferings—Last poem—The One Name and The Adieu (poetry)—Death. 9–34

RURAL SCENES:

The Walk in June,	37
An Evening Meditation,	43
Nature's Resurrection,	45
The Bird's Nest,	46
Gather Violets,	47
To a Dandelion,	48
To a Robin,	50
God is There,	51
The Canadian Farmer,	52
The Return,	54
The Old Sugar-Camp,	57
To a Rabbit,	59
The Old Man,	60
The Fading and the Unfading (prose).	62
On Receipt of some Wild Flowers,	62
The Sick Girl's Dream,	63
The Last Song,	65
An Evening Scene,	66
Autumn Teachings (prose),	68
The Watcher,	69

CONTENTS.

PAGE.

PATRIOTIC POEMS:

The Surrender of Quebec,	71
Song of the English Peasant Girl,	82
A Nation's Desire,	83
Canada's Welcome,	84
Our Native Land,	84
The Appeal,	86
I Love the Land where I was Born,	87
The World to Come,	89

TEMPERANCE:

A Welcome to a Temperance Picnic,	92
A Life-Scene—The Letter,	93
The Pledge,	95

SIGHS ON MORTALITY:

What is Your Life?	101
Life,	102
The Silent Army,	104
The Dying Warrior,	106
On Seeing a Skull (prose),	107
Thoughts on Death,	108
The Battle-Field,	111
Dead and Forgot,	112
Dear Emily,	114
On the Death of a Friend (prose),	115
The Heavenly Helper,	116
The Promise,	118
The Dead Christ (prose),	120
The Complaint,	120
The Mixed Cup (prose),	122
I Shall Depart,	122
Time Flies,	124
A Voice from the Sick Room (prose),	125

PAGE.

Songs of Hope:

"He Giveth Songs in the Night,"	130
The Last Good Night,	131
Retrospective and Prospective (prose),	132
Hope,	132
Earth Not the Christian's Home,	133
"We Sorrow Not as Others Without Hope" (prose),	136
The Messenger Bird,	137
Our Ship is Homeward Bound,	138
Midnight,	140
Easter Sunday (prose),	141
The Risen Redeemer (prose),	142
Dost Thou Remember Me?	143
"'T is I—Be Not Afraid,"	144
The Only Perfect One (prose),	145
The Dying Christian,	146
The Request,	147
Complete in Him (prose),	148
Trust in God,	149
A Paradox (prose),	150
"Thou Shalt Know Hereafter,"	151
Thine Eyes Shall See the King in His Beauty (prose),	152
All Is Well,	153
We Shall Meet,	154
What the Daughter of the Cloud Said (prose),	155
This is not Home,	156
The Soul's Consolation (prose),	157
"We See through a Glass Darkly,"	158
Words of Cheer for Fainting Christians (prose),	159

Miscellany:

The Dying Year,	162
Incomprehensibility of God,	162
The Star of Bethlehem,	163
God Made Me Poor,	164

CONTENTS.

	PAGE.
The Stranger Guest,	165
A Long, Delightful Walk (prose),	166
"The Servant is Not Above his Master,"	167
Elijah,	169
The Sacred Page,	171
Behold how He Loved Us,	172
Love Your Enemies,	174
The Orphan,	175
Sententious Paragraphs (prose),	178
"Ye Did It Not to Me,"	179
Hear and Help Me,	180
Farewell,	181
No Mother,	182
To a Mother on the Death of her Child,	183
In Goodness is True Greatness,	184
Similes (prose),	185
The Crucified of Galilee,	187
The Ascension,	188
The Hebrew's Lament,	190
When Shall I Receive my Diploma? (prose),	191
Alone with Jesus,	192
The Lost Babe,	194
The Day of Wrath,	195
The Believer's Safety (prose),	197

Life Sketch.

THE hill country of Judea, which furnished a home for the virgin mother of our Lord, is not the only rural region from whence have come women endowed with intelligence and integrity, philanthropy and religion, who by pen and tongue have brightened and blest the hearts and homes of thousands. Nurtured amidst the wilds of nature, instead of the bustle and bewildering attractions of city life, they have grown strong to do battle for the right and to bear testimony to the truth as it is in Jesus. Of this class is the one whose life and labors we are now to consider.

Memphremagog is an enchanting lake, two-thirds of which lie in the Eastern Townships of Canada, in the Province of Quebec, and the upper third in Vermont. Its extreme length from north to south is about thirty miles, its breadth varying from one to three miles. It is semi-circular in form and bestudded with islands; while on its western shore rise mountains of no ordinary attractions, among them Owl's Head, which towers about 2,500 feet above the surface of the lake, affording from its summit a panoramic view of surpassing loveliness. It was at "The Outlet" of this lake there was born, Oct. 27, 1834, HELEN MAR, the youngest daughter of Abel B. and

Polly Johnson; and there she spent—with the exception of the time devoted to attending or teaching school—almost her entire life. Of cities she knew nothing by experience; but as her reading was extensive she knew much of the world by mental surveys. The book of Nature was her delight. Its illustrations of stones and streams, lakes and rivers, mountains and forests, birds and flowers, were ever attractive to her. At an early age she began to exhibit rare poetic talent. Of "a number of short pieces, written between the ages of twelve and fifteen years," the following, entitled "The Forest," has been preserved. It appeared in the *Stanstead Journal*—a paper to which she afterwards frequently contributed. It was probably the first article she ever had printed.

"Let others seek sweet friendship's voice
 When grief the spirit bends,
Let them find solace in the tones
 Of their beloved friends;
But oh! when sorrow o'er me broods,
Give me the dark, the dark green woods.

"When pleasure lights the sparkling eye,
 And swells with rapture proud,
Let others spend their joyous mirth
 Within the giddy crowd;
But when o'er me no clouds are seen,
Give me the forest, dark and green.

"When pure devotion fills the heart,
 And breathes a yearning prayer,
Let others wander to the church
 And pay their tribute there;
But if o'er me such feelings steal,
In the dark forest let me kneel.

"When death comes o'er the pallid brow
 To number with the dead,

> Let others choose some lovely grave,
>   Where tears will oft be shed;
> But let me, let me find a tomb
>   Deep in the forest's darkening gloom."

Her life was not one of thrilling adventure, hairbreadth escapes, and deeds securing worldly applause, but quiet, unobtrusive and useful. Her constitution was naturally weak—her brain too active for her body, and as a consequence much mental and physical suffering was her portion. To her studies—French, Latin and drawing, besides the English branches—she was very devoted. Nothing pleased her better than to be alone with books, pen and pencil, or to wander forth in garden or field. Being of a very bashful and retiring disposition she felt alone even in company. Her diary leaves give evidence of this. Under date of June 19, 1852, for example, she writes:

"How lonely I feel to-day! and my rebellious heart will repeat the question, Why was I created thus? I stand alone, and why? I know it is my own self that makes me so; but how can I make myself otherwise? I have tried very, *very* hard to overcome my—what shall I call it? bashfulness? It seems as though it could not be wholly that. I have seen those the world called *bashful*, but they were not at all like myself. Oh, no; I am wretched at times on account of this ——. When I see myself all alone —different from those around me—I cannot stay the burning tear though I would gladly repress it. I cannot soothe the anguish that fills my heart, and yet I feel that this is wrong,—that it ought not to be thus. Why should I feel so keenly that I am *alone?* that I am strange? Earthly scenes will soon be over, and if I am only a Christian I shall never feel alone in heaven. Oh, glorious thought! there will be no strange being there. O God, prepare me for that blissful world and I will no longer complain of my loneliness on earth—no longer sigh that I am not like others."

At this time Miss JOHNSON was not a professed Christian. Her parents had endeavored to bring her up in the fear of the Lord and a belief of the gospel, and to attend the services of the sanctuary. Her life had been one of strict morality. She believed in God but had not taken Christ as *her own personal Saviour* and confessed him before men as she felt she should. Her conviction of sin however was deep and pungent. On another day in the same month, she says:—

"O Earth, thou art a lovely place, and some of thy inhabitants are as lovely and happy as thyself. See that beautiful bird, with shining plumage and brilliant crest, and hear the melodious notes that arise from its silvery throat! Its form proclaims beauty, and its song happiness. See those snow-white lambs skipping over the verdant grass,—now nestling sportively beside their bleating mothers, then springing forward, bounding from knoll to knoll, and filling the air with strains of joy and delight! See yonder butterfly weighing itself upon that brilliant flower: his gorgeous wings are expanded and glittering in the sun like sparkling gems! See those bright-eyed children! their glowing cheeks, their beaming eyes, and above all their clear and merry laugh proclaiming happiness pure and unbounded. Earth is truly lovely, but its inhabitants are not all happy. Oh no, not *all*, for one who loves the beauties of earth, rejoices in the loveliness of nature, and finds her chief pleasures in the spreading grove, by the babbling brook, among the brilliant flowers, is sad and unhappy. And why? Because she has learned too soon that there is no such thing as [real and abiding] happiness on earth, that the fairest plants wither, that pleasure is a deceitful phantom—false and fleeting. Truly she has learned all this, and will she *never* learn to raise her eyes to that bright world where true happiness only resides, and to trust meekly in Him who is the only Dispenser of peace and joy?"

Later we have another entry in which, after again referring to the beauties of nature, she exclaims:

"O life, life! I fain would read thy mysteries: I fain would draw aside every vail and behold for what purpose I was created. Was it to be an heir of sorrow? was it to live for myself alone, and then pass away and let my memory perish with me? No, I was born for a better—a higher and more holy purpose. I was not born to pass a few moments on the stage of life and then disappear forever. . . . . With a shudder I turn away and would gladly forget to think. O thought, thought! thou wilt distract me,—thou hast almost hurled reason from her throne. Thou bitter tormentor! depart, if but for a moment, and let me once more find peace. But no; the more I seek to elude still nearer the demon pursues. O thought, thought! it rushes forth from my soul like the wild outpourings of the volcanic mountains and overwhelms me with its burning tide till body, mind and soul— all, all are exhausted and lie like a straw upon the roaring bosom of the deep. Oh, that I could arise, mingle with the gay, and forget my own deep and overpowering thoughts. But no; such thoughts, like the soul which gave them birth, can never die. O thought, what art thou? A blessing to angels, a curse to me. Distracted soul, sink into repose: others are happy, and wast thou born to be more wretched than they? Truly thou wast, and why? Because thou livest only in the regions of thought—*thought* which is burning my brain and piercing my lacerated heart. And yet a thought freighted with light beams through the dark clouds which its darker sisters have thrown around me, and the only inscription which it bears is, '*Live for others.*' And another thought follows in rapid succession,—like a far-off echo it repeats the words of its predecessor, '*Live for others*,' and then adds (while a vivid flash of the lightning of truth lights up the darkness of error), '*Live for God and for heaven.*' A loud crash follows. Peals of thunder shake the atmosphere of my soul! *Self* has fallen: *I will live for others, for God and for heaven.*"

This was a grand resolve; but not yet was the soul to be out of prison, the pilgrim to be freed from the Slough of Despond. Once more she has to write:—

"Everything is beautiful, and all nature is glad and rejoicing. Arise, my soul, and be thou glad likewise. Cast off thy gloomy fears. The God who made all the beautiful things by which thou art surrounded is not unmindful of thee. Oh, wondrous condescension! God is not forgetful of *me*. He gazes upon me with an eye of compassion; he pities my distress and my weakness. Amazing love! Oh, that I were more worthy of it; Oh, that I loved him as fervently as I ought! But my heart is callous, and I am nothing but a poor, cold, vile and helpless sinner: nothing but sin *dwells* in my heart. It is the seat of every vice, every evil thought, and every depraved passion. [Jer. 17:9, 10; Mark 7:21–23]. Dark and gloomy clouds envelope my soul. A weight of sorrow presses upon my heart, and I vainly strive to free myself from its influence. Everything looks dark. 'My God, my God, why hast thou forsaken me? why art thou so far from helping me?' 'How long wilt thou forget me, O Lord? forever? How long wilt thou hide thy face from me?' 'Mine iniquities are gone over my head: as a heavy burden they are too heavy for me. Lord, all my desire is before thee; and my groaning is not hid from thee. Make haste to help me.' 'My soul fainteth for thy salvation, but I hope in thy word.' O my God, hear my cry, and answer my petition."

"*Tuesday, June* 29, 1852. The sultry fires of the day have yielded to the cool breezes of evening. A misty cloud hangs over the once azure sky, and the deep, heavy roar of thunder shakes the quiet air. Nearer and nearer still it rolls its deep-toned voice, and all nature seems to reply. The vivid lightnings flash. The fountains on high are opened, and the rain pours down in torrents. Wilder grows the storm: the winds are released from their 'prison-cave,' and armed with fury they rush madly forth; brighter the lightnings glare, louder the thunders roar. The whole fabric of nature seems in commotion! Oh, who can gaze upon such a scene without emotions of awe, wonder and admiration? Surely such an one must possess a stony heart and a cold nature. There is beauty for me in the lightning's glare—there is music in the thunder's peal! God grant that there may be beauty and glory for me in the day when the thundering notes of the last trumpet shall shake the heavens and awaken the sleeping dead,—when 'the elements shall melt with fervent heat,' and every soul of every tribe, and tongue and nation shall stand before the judgment-seat to receive their final doom! O grant that the Judge may be my friend, and that I—the poorest, the lowest, the vilest of sinners—may find a seat at his right hand; and the vaults of heaven shall forever ring with the praises of a redeemed sinner, saved only through the grace and blood of the crucified Saviour."

But the hour was at hand when there was to come such relief to the troubled soul as it had never before experienced,—when the divine Comforter was to take of the things of Christ and reveal them to the longing heart,—and this maiden avow herself before the world a disciple of Christ. How was this to be effected?

Sunday, July 25, I had an appointment to preach in Magog, and after the forenoon service expected to baptize a young lady who had been a schoolmate of Miss JOHNSON. In view of that arrangement I urged that they should both go together in the ordinance, but could get no encouragement that it would be so. We went to the church, where I preached from Col. 3 : 1–4, and after sermon announced the hymn,—

"Gracious Lord, incline thine ear,
My request vouchsafe to hear;
Burdened with my sins, I cry,
Give me Christ, or else I die.

* * * * * * * *

Father, thou hast given thy Son,
Bruised for sins that I have done;
To that refuge now I fly;
Christ is mine—I shall not die."

The effect and what followed I will allow her to relate in her own words:—

"Oh, the *agony* and the *perfect peace* that I have this day enjoyed! The agony in the morning was almost insupportable. It seemed then utterly impossible for me to take up so heavy a cross as to follow my Saviour in the ordinance of baptism. The very thought was dreadful, and yet I knew that it was my duty. I felt that the anger of God would be kindled against me,—that his Holy Spirit would not always strive with me. I threw myself upon my knees; but could find no peace there as long as I continued proudly obstinate. I started from my knees and seized 'the holy Book of God'; but there was nothing there to comfort me. I paced the room hurriedly, at every step exclaiming, 'What shall I do?' and yet I knew what to do, but would not do it. Thus the morning passed away, and trembling with emotion I entered the house of God. The sermon seemed designed expressly for me. At its close I grew more agitated. The last hymn was read, and after singing we were to repair to the water, where one happy being was to follow her blessed Saviour into a watery grave. Oh, I shall never forget that hymn,— never, no never. The closing line of each verse seemed as an echo from my own heart, 'Give me Christ or else I die'; but as the last line of the last verse fell upon my ear—'*Christ is mine, I shall not die,*"—I think that then I did truly feel determined to come boldly forth and claim the precious promises of God *as my own*.

"We sought the water's side, when Josephine asked me in a trembling voice if I would be baptized. I thought she expected an answer in the negative— at least I knew that she might reasonably expect it, for I had told her plainly in the morning that I could not. My heart was too full to speak: I only bowed my head in token of assent. I shall never forget the look of joy that beamed in her countenance, nor the emotions that filled my own bosom. I saw Eliza enter the water. Oh, glorious sight! I never saw, never imagined so beautiful a scene. Every fear vanished, every cloud withdrew from my soul, and I *longed* to enter the waving flood. O my Saviour! I did not enter it alone. Surely it was nothing short of the almighty arm of God that supported me then. I never in all my life had so little fear of man : I had *no fear* then. Truly it was a foretaste of heaven. Oh, happy, thrice happy moment! it was worth a whole lifetime of sorrow. If I could always feel as I did then my heart would never again be bowed down with grief: but that very afternoon Satan began to whisper : 'You will not live up to your profession; you have deceived yourself and others; you are still a wicked creature ; you are not a Christian '; and yet by the grace of God I was able, in some degree at least, to resist him.

"When I partook of the Lord's supper I felt a repetition of the happiness I had while obeying the command of my Saviour and following him into a watery grave. How vividly the last supper which Christ partook of with his disciples presented itself to my mind! and then I looked forward with joyful hope to the day when all the saints of God shall eat bread in his glorious kingdom,—when all of every age and clime shall be gathered around the table, and Jesus Christ himself be in their midst. It was a soul-inspiring thought, and for all the wealth of a thousand worlds like this I would not have been absent from that communion—from which I had so often absented myself. Yes; I had never before partaken of the Lord's supper; and it was my own wicked heart which had kept me away, for God had called loudly upon me, and his Holy Spirit had again and again striven with me. Oh, what a sinner I have been, and what a longsuffering God! I wonder that he did not cast me off forever. Oh, what mercy! 'Bless the Lord, O my soul, and all that is within me bless his holy name. Bless the Lord, O my soul, and forget not all his benefits.' And now, have I forsaken all for Christ? Have I thrown myself—body, soul and spirit—upon the altar? I do want to sacrifice everything for Christ, and *by the grace of God* I will perform the following:—

"1. When my duty appears plain I will do it, whatever may be the consequences.

"2. I will never be ashamed to confess Christ before the world.

"3. I will consecrate my talents entirely to the Lord.

"4. I will never employ my pen in writing anything which I might regret at the bar of God.

"5. I will never permit any one of my compositions to be printed unless I can in sincerity ask the blessing of God to attend it.

"6. As I shall be brought into judgment for every idle word I say, I will endeavor never to engage in trifling conversation, but on every proper occasion to speak of the wondrous grace of God.

"7. I will, whenever a good opportunity occurs, warn my young companions to flee from the wrath to come.

"8. I will strive to set my affections on things above, not on things on the earth.

"9. By the assistance of the Holy Spirit I will endeavor to keep evil thoughts out of my heart, and to meditate upon the law of God.

"10. I will never pass a day without seeking some secret place at least twice a day, and pouring out my soul in prayer to God.

"11. I will study the Holy Scriptures, and endeavor to understand what I read.

"12. I will try to do all I can.

"O God, assist me to perform what I have written in thy fear and to thy glory. I am perfect weakness: but 'thou knowest my frame, thou rememberest that I am dust.' I know thou art merciful; Oh, give me a more exalted faith. Help me to come boldly forward and claim thy promises as mine. Humble my pride; keep me at thy feet; let not the temptations of Satan overcome me, but may I trust myself in thine arms. May I love thee fervently, above everything else—better far than my own life. I can do nothing unless thou dost assist me. Oh, support me, and save me at last in thy kingdom, for Christ's sake."

In the evening of that ever memorable Sabbath she offered aloud a few words of prayer at the family altar, and next day (as she was then teaching) had prayer in her school: thus she "confessed with the mouth the Lord Jesus" while in her heart she believed that God had raised him from the dead (Rom. 10 : 9). Immediately after the Son of God himself was baptized, he was in the wilderness "tempted of the devil"; it need not be thought strange therefore if his followers soon after their baptism are also grievously assaulted by the same adversary. This young Christian did not escape him entirely; yet from that day until her death, though conscious of much weakness and imperfection, having many dark days and great sufferings, she never renounced her allegiance to the King of kings, who had bought her with his blood. A few more selections from her diary will show the working of her mind about this time.

"*Aug.* 7. A calm and quiet morning. A soothing calm steals over my soul. Faith, with triumphant wing, rises far above the scenes of earth and points to that glorious world where Christ pleads for me before the throne of his Father. The doubts which have so long filled my heart are sinful and dishonoring to God, and I will no longer give place to them: I will look away from myself—from my sins—to the holy Lamb of God. I will trust wholly in him and in his merits alone for acceptance."

"*Sunday, Aug.* 8. What I have done to-day would once have seemed impossible, the cross that I have taken up would have seemed almost insupportable. I could not have believed the last time I attended the prayer-meeting that at the next one I should stand up as a witness for Christ. But thank God! my proud heart has in some degree been humbled, and the dearest hope I now cherish is, that Christ may not be ashamed to confess me before his Father and all the holy angels."

"*Aug.* 22. While standing this evening by the grave of one dearly beloved in life, and cherished more fondly now that death has taken her from my embrace, I could not stay the soaring flight of fancy, which would portray to my mind in vivid colors our meeting at the great Resurrection morn; and the thought that that meeting was so near—that in a very little while the grave should lose its power and that she would come forth robed in immortal beauty, filled my soul with transport and almost brought to my lips the yearning cry, 'Come, Lord Jesus, and come quickly.'"

On the 27th of August Miss JOHNSON closed her

school, and after spending a few weeks at home went to the academy at Derby Centre, Vt. Under date of "Wednesday, Oct. 26," we have this entry in her journal:—

"Attended the exercises to-night and read a composition. They could not have liked it, for it was upon a subject which must be disagreeable to the world; and yet it is the subject nearest my heart—one that I love to dwell upon and to hear about: the coming of my blessed Saviour. When will the glorious morn appear! Loud and repeated cheers were given when Miss —— read her composition. Well, it was good; such as would suit the world, but not *me*—strange being that I am. But I shall not always be so: in heaven I shall not be a stranger. There I can converse with the saints dearly-beloved: for their conversation will be on the things of God; and my Saviour himself will deign to address me there! Why should I not then long, aye *long* to obtain that blissful state? And yet I sometimes fear that I shall fall far short of it, for I am so vile and polluted."

The "composition" referred to we do not find among her papers; but much that she has written shows that she was indeed deeply interested in "that blessed hope" (Tit. 2 : 13). She was a decided premillennialist, and stood identified in her church-membership with the Evangelical Adventists. On completing her eighteenth year (Oct. 27, 1852), she said:—

"This evening, while looking back through all the events of my life, what is there that rejoices me most? It is one that the past year has brought forth,—one that will ever be remembered with deep and powerful emotions: the day that consecrated me to the Lord, when I breathed forth with a fervent heart, 'Give me Christ, or else I die,' and I was enabled to take up my cross and follow my Saviour in baptism."

Here there is no regret expressed for the step she had taken, nor did she ever feel any, though she greatly deplored her weakness and unprofitableness in the Lord's service. And why not? Listen to her, under date of June 13, 1853:—

"How sweet, when the soul has no earthly support, to fly to the Rock of Ages! The Saviour is precious to the heart of the pardoned sinner. There is nothing like the love of Jesus. He is not like other friends—oftentimes wearied by our complaints and the repetition of our sorrows, but is always longsuffering and delighting to hear and answer every cry of the burdened spirit; smiling ever in the darkest of afflictions, and forever dropping the balm of consolation into the distracted breast. Oh, what a privilege to have such a friend—such a sure and steadfast friend —such a wise and omnipotent friend. And he is *my* friend? Yes; he is '*the sinner's* FRIEND,' and therefore mine: for surely nothing but wondrous *love* could have led him to die a cruel and ignominious death for *me*, polluted as I am. O Jesus, thou art my friend and I will be thy friend; thou didst love me first and I do love thee, but not as fervently as I should, nor so much as I desire. O God, give me more of thy Holy Spirit; may it consume every unhallowed passion, tear every idol from my heart, and consecrate that heart entirely to thee."

The only journal notes of considerable length which Miss JOHNSON seems to have made were for the years 1852 and 1853. Those for 1855 and 1860 were entered in a "daily miniature diary." We find none for other years, though she always kept her pen and pencil busy in some way as long as she had strength to write. The diary for 1855 is in rhyme—usually six lines being allotted to each day. While some of the verses are playful and witty, most of them are religious and plaintive. The following are given as specimens:

> "Arose at six o'clock today:
> How swift the moments sped away
>   Engaged in household duties;
> Then Virgil claimed awhile my care,
> And Pope of time a larger share,
>   With all his sweets and beauties."

> "Mr. Goodenough and wife
>   Came here yesterday;
> Through the changing scenes of life
>   Onward be their way;
> And never may their path be rough
> So long as they are Good-enough."

> "Received of Robinson to-day
> For my 'Address' a little pay:
> The first of cash I ever had
> For writing verses, good or bad.
> O Lord, whate'er my gains may be
> The tenth I dedicate to thee."

> "I would not seek the haunts of mirth,
> For in the gayest scenes of earth
>   Are hovering grief and care;
> But oft I find a soothing power,
> At twilight's calm and peaceful hour,
>   In secret prayer."

> "Jesus, oh, precious name!
>   How sweet it sounds to me;
> Come want, come grief, come death or shame
>   I'll cling, my Lord, to thee."

"I'd rather be distressed with doubts
  And find no sweet release,
Than be content to settle down
  In false repose and peace;
But, ah! I wish I knew my name
In the Lamb's book a place could claim."

"While here distressed I lie,
  What joy my heart doth thrill
At the enchanting thought,
  That Jesus loves me still!"

"Sweet Sabbath morn! to me it brings,
As if on angel's airy wings,
  Visions of peace and rest:
I seem to stand upon the plains
Where an eternal Sabbath reigns,
  And dwell the pure and blest.

"I wept—when lo, my heart to cheer
J—— sobbing whispered in my ear:
'Dont cry, for I will serve the Lord ;'
How sweet the sound! what great reward."
                    [*Psa.* 126 : 5, 6].

"How little comfort have I known
  In this dark vale of tears!
For Sorrow marked me for her own
  In childhood's early years,
And ever since, by night and day,
Has hovered round my lonely way."

"'Twas nearly two—but sleep had fled
  My pillow for the night;
I rose—but all was dark around,
  And I could find no light:
And then I knelt and prayed for those
Who, like me, found no sweet repose."

"Sick, sick, sick,
  And gloomy all the day;
Sick, sick, sick,
  Thus life wears away."

"Murmur not, my troubled soul,
　At thy Father's dealings;
Wild the billows round thee roll:
　Yield not to the feelings
Of despair that gather round:
Troubles rise not from the ground."
　　　　　　　　　　　[*Job* 5 : 6–8].

"How many souls around the throne
　Once suffered here like me,—
Like me discouraged, tempted, tried,
　But now for ever free:
They shout their griefs and trials o'er;
Then let me fear and doubt no more."

"At home all day; I cannot pray,
　Can neither read nor think:
O God, I cry; the waves roll high,
　Support me or I sink."

"Did I murmur that the rod
　Was so heavy, O my God?
I forgot the cursed tree,
I forgot Gethsemane.
I forgot the grief and pain—
May I ne'er forget again."

"Unworthy, wretched as I am
　I hope for mercy through the Lamb:
His name, his glorious name prevails
　When every other passport fails;
It opens Heaven's eternal gate;
Then, doubting soul, why longer wait?"

"Sabbath after Sabbath comes;
　When will dawn the endless day?
Swiftly roll the wheels of time,
　Swiftly pass the hours away;
Brighter and brighter from afar
View we now 'the Morning Star.'"

"And we, alas! are called to part:
　'Farewell' is said, with aching heart;
But God will watch o'er thee I ween,

And guide thee through each trying scene,
My dearest sister Josephine!"

"The glorious sun
　His race has run,
And sweetly sought repose:
　O that for me
　This life might be
As bright—as calm its close!"

"What an awful peal of thunder!
O my soul, be still and wonder;
Yet another, and another—
Each one louder than the other;
God of heaven, I *see* thy power,
May I *feel* it hour by hour."

"A thousand twinkling stars to-night
Look down with soft and silvery light
And tell the majesty divine
Of Him who gives them leave to shine.
Oh, what an atom must I be,
And yet He loves and cares for me!"

"The wheels of Time—how swift they roll!
Dost thou consider, O my soul,
That it shall soon be said to thee:
' Time was, but time no more shall be ' ?
Then seize upon the present hour;
Improve it to thy utmost power."

In the fall of 1856 Miss Johnson was prostrated by disease, and nearly all the time afterwards confined to the house. So numerous and complicated were her difficulties as to baffle the skill of all the physicians who saw her, and no one knows the amount of suffering she endured. Her mind however was active and vigorous, and though there were seasons—sometimes quite protracted—when to her the heavens above seemed as brass and the earth iron, yet God did not forsake her: the sunshine succeeded the storm, and the peace that Jesus gives was poured into her wounded heart. Referring to her afflictions in 1858 and the two following years she writes:—

"Those were days and nights of anguish, but I now look back to them with feelings of regret, for my feet had only touched the dark waters and my lips had only tasted the cup from which I was to drink the very dregs. Early in the spring of 1858 I was seized with fever and acute inflammation of the stomach, which brought me to the verge of the grave. I could feel the warm tears of beloved ones upon my cheeks, as they bent tenderly over me; I could see the dark vale just ahead (though there was a light amid the darkness), but my sufferings were not to be so soon terminated. Gradually my disease assumed a chronic form, and physicians said there was no hope. The little nourishment I could take distressed me so terribly that the very thought of eating made me shudder, and my stomach became so sore that I could not be moved from one side of the bed to the other without uttering a cry of pain. Winter, spring, summer and autumn in turn visited the earth, and with each I thought, aye, longed to depart; but the great Refiner had his own purpose to accomplish,—there was a little fine gold but the dross rendered it useless. The ordeal through which I am passing is indeed a terrible one, but I know where peace and consolation are to be found, and there are times when I can say in sincerity, 'Thy will be done.'"

Thursday, Jan. 1, 1863, she wrote:—

"Bright, beautiful day. Many people on the ice. Edwin [her brother] there. Over our dwelling is a shadow; it falls upon our spirits and we are sad.

Will it never be removed? God grant we may be patient and grateful for the blessings we do enjoy, for are not friends—true, tender friends, the greatest and holiest of blessings? and while we have them God forgive us for murmuring at his dealings."

The last entries in her diary are: "Feb. 2. Very sick"; "Tuesday, 3rd. No better." It is uncertain when the following lines were written, but it might have been about this time :—

> "I'm going home to that bright land of rest
> Where pain and grief and sickness are unknown;
> The year begins in sorrow, but will close
> In joys that never end—I'm going home!
> Last year the warning came on sunken eye
> And wasted cheek. I gazed and thought to spend
> My Christmas with the angels. God knows best;
> And here I linger, weary sufferer still.
> The morning comes long watched-for, long desired;
> The day drags on, and then the sleepless night:
> But this will have an end—it must be soon."

About six weeks before her death she was taken with nausea and vomiting: everything she took distressed her, and for the last twenty-three days she took no nourishment save what water contains. Her prayer—

> "Close to the Cross, close to the Cross, God grant I may be found
> When death shall call my spirit hence, or the last trumpet sound,"—

was indeed answered. Her end was very peaceful and happy. For several weeks not a cloud seemed to pass over her mind; and though often in great distress there was no impatience manifested, nor did a murmur escape her lips. She said, "It is nothing to die : 'the sting of death is sin,' and when sin is taken away the sting is gone." On another occasion she remarked: "I have often heard the words sung—

> 'Jesus can make a dying bed
> Feel soft as downy pillows are'—

and thought they were not strictly true; but now I know that they are perfectly, *perfectly* so." Once as we stood by her bedside she observed her mother and sister weeping, and with a countenance beaming with joy (sufficient to remind us of 1 Pet. 1 : 8) she expressed surprise, remarking: "It seems to me I am only crossing a narrow brook, and as I look back I see you all coming—we shall soon meet." Her view of her own weakness and sinfulness was indeed clear, but she had such unwavering faith in her Redeemer as enabled her to say : "Dying seems to me like laying the head back and closing the eyes, just to open them in a few moments on the joys of paradise." The following lines, written with a pencil on the cover and blank leaf of her French Testament, were the last she ever wrote. They are dated March 3—just ten days before her death—and give indubitable evidence of the clearness of her intellect and the strength of her faith while passing through " the valley of the shadow of death " :—

> " Jesus, I know thou art the living Word!
> Each blessed promise to myself I take;
> I would not doubt, if I had only heard
> This—this alone, '*I never will forsake!*'
>
> I have no fear—the sting of death is sin,
> And Christ removed it when he died for me:

Washed in his blood, my robe without, within,
Has not a stain that God himself can see.

Wrapped in the Saviour's arms I sweetly lie;
Far, far behind I hear the breakers roar;
I have been dying—but I cease to die,
My rest begins—rejoice forevermore!"

Having expressed a wish to be visited by all her acquaintances, many called to see her, with whom she conversed freely on the interests of their soul. With great composure she made arrangements for her departure—leaving books and other articles to her intimate friends. One day she made a request that I should preach her funeral sermon. For a moment I hesitated because of relationship (having married her sister Josephine), then remarked, that I supposed there would be no impropriety in doing so, as I recollected that Whitefield preached his wife's, to which she immediately added, "And Wesley preached his mother's." On asking if she had thought of any passage to be used as a text, she replied: "I first thought of the words, 'I shall be satisfied, when I awake, with thy likeness'; but you know that is all about *I*, and now I feel that Christ is all—it is all Christ: so I have thought of his words in the 11th of John, 'I am the Resurrection and the Life.'" She also suggested to her sister that the following hymns (which were favorites with her) should be used on the occasion:

" Come let us join our cheerful songs
   With angels round the throne;"

" On Jordan's stormy banks I stand
   And cast a wishful eye,"—

"Joyfully, joyfully, onward I move,
Bound for the land of bright glory and love."

The joyous character of the hymns will at once be noted; and this was the very reason why she selected them: she considered that they would be more expressive of her condition than the mournful ones which are so frequently used at funerals. Two of her poems seem so appropriate here that we insert them. The former was written in June, 1859, and the latter bears date "Nov. 30, 1861":—

THE ONE NAME.—ACTS 4 : 12.

"When round my dying bed ye stand,
And kiss my cheek and clasp my hand,
Oh, whisper in my failing ear
The only Name I care to hear,—
The only Name that has the power
To comfort in the dying hour.

"Let neither sob nor sigh be heard,
But still repeat that sacred word,—
Until the solace it imparts
Descends like balm upon your hearts,
And I in triumph gladly sing:
'O dreaded Death, where is thy sting?'

"And when released from sin and clay
My happy spirit soars away,
And pauses at the heavenly gate,
Where saints and smiling angels wait,
And views the city bright and fair,—
That Name shall be my passport there!

"Oh then, in calm and holy trust,
Give my poor body to the dust—
Assured that God will guard the clay
Until the Resurrection Day,
When he on whom my soul relies
In thunder tones will bid me rise.

LIFE-SKETCH.

"Amid the earth-devouring storm,
　Made like my Saviour's glorious form,
　Redeemed from sickness, death, and pain,
　I shall awake to life again;
　And soul and body both shall be
　With Christ throughout eternity."

THE ADIEU.

"You will miss me when I am gone—
　At morning, at night, and noon:
　I have needed your arm to lean upon,
　I shall need it no longer soon.

"I've been helpless for many years,
　'No *burden*' you always said;—
　I have claimed your pity, your prayers and tears
　You will miss me when I am dead.

"How many a dreary night
　You have watched by my couch of pain,
　Till the streaming in of morning light—
　You will never watch again.

"God taketh not all away
　The bitter and sweet he blends,
　And I bless his name by night and day
　That he has not denied me friends.

"You have shared the heavy load,
　Which alone I could not have borne;
　I am going now to a bright abode,
　But I leave you, alas! to mourn.

"You will miss me when I am gone,
　As you never have missed before!
　I have needed your arm to lean upon
　But soon I shall need it no more.

"I lean on my Saviour's breast
　In this hour of mortal pain;
　Oh, strong are His arms! and sweet my rest!
　Farewell! till we meet again."

The expected hour though long of coming arrived at last. As long as she seemed to realize what was transpiring around her, and when too weak to converse, she would signify by a word or motion that she had peace and all was well. About a quarter past 11 o'clock Friday night, March 13, 1863, "the silver cord was loosed," and she sweetly fell asleep in Jesus, aged twenty-eight years, four months, and sixteen days. On the Tuesday following we buried her from the village church, where ten years before she had decided to come out openly on the Lord's side. It was crowded. Three ministers, from as many different denominations, assisted me in the services. Her mother and sister (the wife of Dr. G. O. Somers) were too feeble to attend. But we hope soon to greet her where—to use her own words,

> "Earthly love is like the starlight lost
> In glorious sunshine, and the things of time
> Shrink into nothing: even death itself
> Fades like a shadow in the noontide blaze,
> And life—new, glorious, everlasting life—
> Expands the soul, and all it ever dreamed
> Of heavenly bliss becomes reality."

Above the stillness of death we hear the words of inspiration: "Precious in the sight of the Lord is the death of his saints"; "Thy dead shall live again"; and in hope we wait. The weary pilgrim has reached her resting-place. She lies in the chamber of Peace, whose windows open toward the sunrising.

Thou King of kings, Almighty One!
  bend unto me the ear
That listens to the music
  of every rolling sphere,
And guide, oh guide my feeble hand
  to strike my slumbering lyre
To strains harmonious and divine,
  and every thought inspire.
—*Poems, p.* 9.

Rural Scenes.

THE WALK IN JUNE.

A walk in June, in early June,
    Our sweet Canadian June—
When every tree is all in leaf,
    And every bird in tune;
When laughing rills leap down the hills
    And through the meadows play,
Inviting to their verdant banks
    The old, the young, the gay.

When not a cloud is in the sky,
    Nor shadow on the lake
Save what the trees that line the shore
    And little islands make,—
When every nook where'er we look,
    Is bright with dewy flowers,
And violets are thickly strewn
    As though they fell in showers.

How sweetly on the balmy air
    The children's voices ring!
And even I renew my youth
    With each returning spring.
Oh, we may keep a fresh young heart
    Though outward beauty fade,
If we but cherish there a love
    For all that God has made.

I do not call a happy man
    The man that's rich or great;

Nor him who stands with folded hands
  And says, " It is my fate ! "
But he is blest who cheerfully
  Endures or does his part,
And looks on earth, and sea, and sky
  With an adoring heart.

He wanders by the pebbly beach
  And by the summer brook,
And thoughtfully he turns the leaves
  Of Nature's blessed book.
In forest shade, on hill, in vale,
  Where'er he walks abroad,
There goes an humble worshipper—
  A lover of his God.

The cares that trouble other men
  For him have little weight;
He values glory at its worth,
  Nor cringes to the great.
His simple pleasures never fail,
  Nor make his nature cold,—
And though the years may come and go,
  He never can be old.

You call the picture overdrawn—
  But such a man I know;
Whose presence, like the morning sun,
  Dispels each cloud of woe.
And trustingly I cling to him
  As only true love can,—
My comforter, protector, guide,—
  My love, thou art the man !

And you are teaching me to look
  On nature with your eyes ;

The pleasant change within my heart
    Each day I realize.
The world is brighter now to me,
    A holier thing is life
Than even on that happy day
    When first you called me wife.

The trifles that perplexed me then
    Now leave my spirit calm,—
And for the deeper woes of life
    I have a healing balm.
I see the hand of God in all,
    I know that he is just;
And where I cannot understand
    I've learned to wait and trust.

Oh, I remember well the day—
    'Twas in the month of June,
When every tree was all in leaf,
    And every bird in tune,—
We walked together, arm in arm,
    As we are walking now,
But I was young, and Time had left
    No traces on your brow.

I listened with a strange delight
    To every word you said,
And then to hide the burning tears
    I turned away my head.
I dared not trifle with your love,
    Though till that magic hour
I had not cared for aching hearts
    If they but owned my power.

I never felt so vile before—
    So humbled in mine eyes;

I wondered what you saw to love:
    I thought you must despise.
For I was gay, and you were grave,
    And I was vain and proud:
You loved the meadow and the grove,
    And I the laughing crowd.

I told you frankly of my faults,
    You would not hear me through;
You said you were an erring man,
    And earthly angels few.
But would I show my better side?
    And would I deign to bless?
You held my hand—what *could* I do?
    And so I answered, " Yes."

Do I regret it? Nay, my love,
    For were I free as then
The man I chose I still would choose
    Before all other men.
And I would say, For life or death,
    For happiness or woe,
Where'er you dwell there I will dwell,
    Where'er you go, I go.

That was a day, and that a walk
    To be remembered long:
It changed the current of my life,
    And made each thought a song.
There was a glory in the sky,
    A glory on the trees,
And the perfumes of Paradise
    Were poured on every breeze.

I scarcely seemed to walk the earth,
    My spirit was so light;

'Twas easy then to shun the wrong,
  So easy to do right.
New hopes began to bud and bloom
  Like blossoms in the spring,—
My heart o'erflowed with tenderness
  For every living thing.

I was no more the thoughtless girl
  By idle fancy led;
Life seemed to me reality,
  And yet I did not dread
To walk along its roughest path:
  I should not walk alone,—
Another and a better life
  Was blended with mine own.

One blessing more, and then you said
  Our joy would be complete;
Your prayer was answered when I sat
  At the Redeemer's feet.
And deeper, holier grew our love,—
  Our union was to be
Not only for a lifetime here,
  But for eternity.

Thus peacefully we passed along
  Till that eventful day
When all the labor of our hands
  Like chaff was swept away:
We saw our home made desolate,
  Our pleasant cottage sold;
Men called us poor, but we were rich
  In better things than gold.

For we had lived an honest life;
  We could look up and say:

We never wronged a fellow-man,
　　Nor turned the poor away.
We held a treasure in our arms
　　Which every care beguiled;
He never sorrowed, never sinned—
　　For Jesus took the child.

There is a little mound of earth
　　Where, when the spring appears,
We watch the budding violets,
　　And water them with tears.
Oh, it were more than earthly love
　　That soothed a parent's woe
When there we laid our darling down,
　　Full twenty years ago!

Sometimes my heart grows sad and sick
　　When to the past I turn,
And for a sweet and gentle voice
　　To call me *mother* yearn.
I see the silver in my hair,
　　The lines upon your brow,—
And oh, I wish our boy had lived
　　To be our comfort now!

One moment—then the wish is o'er:
　　The sun begins to shine;
I lift my heart in thankfulness,
　　And say, "Thy will is mine."
'Tis true, of poverty and pain
　　We both have had our share,
But do you think in all the world
　　There is a happier pair?

I know the harvest-time is near,—
　　I know the Reaper stands

Before us, and I tremble much
    Lest he unlock our hands.
But God will be our strength and shield,
    Our refuge in that hour;
And he will join our hands again
    Beyond the Reaper's power.

Now let me wipe away those tears;
    Forget my gloomy talk,
And with your own improve the scene
    And sanctify our walk:
So that with Nature's melody
    Our hearts may be in tune,
And send up incense like the flowers
    This pleasant day in June!

AN EVENING MEDITATION.

How softly yonder pale star beams above my head to-night! How beautiful it appears in the azure vault of heaven where twilight holds the connecting link between day and night. Oh, if my soul were freed from its clayey fetters how swiftly it would fly (if such a journey were possible) to the boundaries of that sweet star! Can that fair planet, seemingly so pure and spotless, be inhabited by beings as frail and erring as ourselves? Can there be any sad souls there to-night—any who are weeping over blighted hopes and blasted prospects? It may be so; and yet perchance such a thing as a pang of sorrow and a burning tear are unknown, for it may be *sin* has never entered there. Vain, useless conjectures! But will the veil which hides the scenes of other worlds from our eyes never be withdrawn? .... Surely it is because God is merciful that I have been spared through another day. I cannot forbear wondering that I have been spared so long,—that I have not been cut down as a cumberer of the ground. O God, according to thy loving-kindness preserve me. Grant that I may yet be an humble instrument in thy hand of doing something for the good of thy cause. Forgive my numberless sins and at last receive me to glory.—*July* 20, 1852.

It is a lovely scene; the sun has set,
    But left his glory in the western sky
Where daylight lingers, half regretful yet
    That sombre Night, her sister, draweth nigh,
    And one pale star just looketh from on high :
'Tis neither day nor night, but both have blent
    Their own peculiar charms to please the eye,—
Declining day its sultry heat has spent,
And calm, refreshing night its grateful coolness lent.

The lake is sleeping—on its quiet breast
    Are clouds of every tint the rainbows wear,
Some are in crimson, some in gold are dressed.
    Oh, had I wings, like yonder birds of air,
    How I would love to dip my pinions there,
Then mount exulting to the heavenly gate,—
    A song of love and gratitude to bear
To Him who gives the lowly and the great,
In earth, and sea, and sky, so glorious an estate.

It is the time when angels are abroad
    Upon their work of love and peace to men,—

Commissioned from the dazzling throne of God,
  They come to earth as joyfully as when
  The tidings ran o'er mountain and o'er glen,
" A son is born, a Saviour and a King,"—
  For they have tidings glorious as then,
Since tokens from our risen Lord they bring,
That life has been secured, and death has lost its sting.

The twilight deepens; o'er the distant hill
  A veil is spread of soft and misty grey;
And from the lake, so beautiful and still,
  The images of sunset fade away;
  The twinkling stars come forth in bright array,
Which shunned the splendor of the noontide glare,—
  A holy calm succeeds the bustling day,
And gentle voices stealing through the air,
Proclaim to hearts subdued the hour of grateful prayer.

NATURE'S RESURRECTION.

Hark! it is the robin crying,
  He has heard the voice of Spring;
From the woods the crow is flying,
  And the jay is on the wing.

Slowly now the sun is ranging
  Each day nearer to the west;
All things tell the year is changing,
  Nature wakens from her rest.

Lower sink the snow-drifts daily,
  Half the pasture lands are bare;
And the little streams leap gayly
  From their chains to breathe the air.

While the barren earth rejoices,
    Care-worn mortal, come away,—
Listen to the pleasant voices
    Of the resurrection day.

Dost thou understand the token?
    Nature should not teach in vain
What its gracious Lord hath spoken—
    That the dead shall live again!

THE BIRD'S NEST.

Two robins came in early Spring,—
    When Winter's reign was o'er;
And every morn I heard them sing
    Just by our cottage door.

They built their nest of moss and hay
    Within a maple tree,—
And thither every pleasant day,
    I went to hear and see.

At first whene'er I came they flew,
    Or eyed me in alarm;
But soon my step familiar grew,
    I never did them harm.

One day a louder song I heard,
    With eager cries for food;
And then I helped the mother-bird
    To still her hungry brood.

I always seemed a welcome guest;
    Both old and young I fed,

Then settling down beneath the nest,
    Some pleasant book I read.

I watched them fondly day by day,
    Until their wings were grown;
When suddenly they flew away,
    And left me all alone.

The bitter tears began to start,
    And full of sad regret
I wondered in my simple heart,
    If birds could thus forget!

Ah! many summers have returned,
    And many changes wrought,
Since I the mournful lesson learned,
    In early childhood taught.

And many hopes have taken wings
    On which my heart was set,—
And I have found that *many things
    As well as birds forget!*

GATHER VIOLETS.

Gather violets white and blue,
    Where the southern zephyrs play;
Bring them sparkling with the dew,—
    With the blessed dew of May.

Let me fold them to my breast,
    Emblems sweet of earthly bliss;
Ha! they love to be caressed,
    For they give me kiss for kiss.

How my weary heart doth yearn,
   Touched as by a hand Divine,
While their soft blue eyes they turn
   Full of sympathy to mine!

Do they know how much I sigh
   For the meadows where they grew?
For the forest and the sky,
   Where they caught their azure hue?

There is One who knows it all,—
   To his loving arms I flee:
Oh, he hears my feeblest call,
   And I know he pities me.

He ere long will take my hand
   Saying tenderly, "Arise!"
He will lead me to the land
   Where no blossom ever dies.

TO A DANDELION.

Blessings on thy sunny face,
In my heart thou hast a place,
   Humble Dandelion!
Forms more lovely are around thee,
Purple violets surround thee,—
But I know thy honest heart
Never felt a moment's smart
At another's good or beauty,—
Ever at thy post of duty,
Smiling on the great and small,
Rich and poor, and wishing all
Health, and happiness, and pleasure,
Oh, thou art a golden treasure!

I remember years ago,
How I longed to see thee blow,
    Humble Dandelion !
Through the meadows I would wander,
O'er the verdant pastures yonder,
Filling hands and filling lap,
Till the teacher's rap, rap, rap,
Sounding on the window sash
Dreadful as a thunder crash,
Called me from my world ideal
To a world how sad and real,—
From a laughing sky and brook
To a dull old spelling-book ;
Then with treasures hid securely,
To my seat I crept demurely.

Childhood's careless days are o'er,
Happy school days come no more,
    Humble Dandelion !
Through a desert I am walking,
Hope eluding, pleasure mocking,
Every earthly fountain dry,
Yet when thou didst meet mine eye,
Something like a beam of gladness
Did illuminate my sadness,
And I hail thee as a friend
Come a holiday to spend
By the couch of pain and anguish.
Where I suffer, moan and languish.

When at length I sink to rest,
And the turf is on my breast,
    Humble Dandelion !
Wilt thou when the morning breaketh,
And the balmy spring awaketh,
Bud and blossom at a breath

From the icy arms of death,
Wilt thou smile upon my tomb?
Drawing beauty from the gloom,
Making life less dark and weary,
Making death itself less dreary,
Whispering in a gentle tone
To the mourner sad and lone,
Of a spring-time when the sleeper
Will arise to bless the weeper?

My Father made this beautiful world and gave me a heart to love his works. Oh, may I love Him better than all created things!

The little plat of ground around our house is a great field of instruction and amusement to me. How little do I comprehend of all contained within it! I am glad I was not born in some great city—where Nature had not been so kind and dear a friend.

TO A ROBIN.

Robin Red-breast on the tree,
Do you sing that song for me?

"You are listening it is true,
But I do not sing for you.
Higher yet on tiptoe rise,
Don't you see a pair of eyes
Peeping through the pleasant shade

Which the summer leaves have made?
There they watch me all day long,
Brightening at my cheerful song,
Turning wheresoe'er I go
For the evening meal below.
Dearest mate that ever blest
Happy lover—peaceful nest,—
Guarding well our eggs of blue,
All my songs I sing for you!"

GOD IS THERE.

When the howling winds are high,
And the vivid lightnings fly
  Through the air;—
When the deafening thunders roll,
Peace to thee, O troubled soul—
  God is there!

When the dreary storm is past,
And the promised bow at last—
  Bright and fair—
In the cloudy sky appears,
Smiling still through Nature's tears
  God is there!

When the tender buds unfold
Bright with purple and with gold
  In the air,—
Or, at twilight when they close
Wrapped awhile in sweet repose
  God is there!

Where the robin chants her lay
Sweetly at the dawn of day,

Or with care
Builds her soft and downy nest,
Lulls her little brood to rest,
God is there!

When the countless stars appear,
Ever to the listening ear
They declare:
He who sees the sparrows fall
Made us and supports us all;
God is there!

When the youthful knee is bent,
And to heaven is humbly sent
Grateful prayer,—
Bending from his throne above
Full of tenderness and love
God is there!

Though his arm sustains the spheres
'Tis the sweetest sound he hears—
Child-like prayer;
Seek then oft the peaceful shade:
There our Blessed Saviour prayed—
God is there!

THE CANADIAN FARMER.

How beautiful thou art, my native stream!
Art thou not worthy of a poet's theme?
The Po and Tiber live in ancient lays,
And smaller streams have had their meed of praise,
Art thou less lovely? True, in classic lore
Thou art unknown, and on thy quiet shore
There are no monuments of other times,

No records of the past—its woes or crimes.
The roar of cannon and the clang of arms
Have never shook thy bosom with alarms,
And never has thy calm and peaceful flood
Been stained to crimson with a brother's blood.
The sportsman's rifle only hast thou heard
Scaring the rabbit and the timid bird;
Or may be in the savage days of yore
The wolf and bear have bled upon thy shore.
But rural peace and beauty reign to-night;
The harvest moon illumes with holy light
Each wave that ripples in its onward flow
O'er rock concealed amid the depths below,
And gives a strange, wild beauty to the scene
On either shore, where trees of evergreen,
Hemlocks and firs, their dusky shadows fling,
Around whose trunks the heavy mosses cling,
With maples clad in crimson, gold and brown,
Bright like the west when first the sun goes down.

Here from this summit where I often roam
I can behold my cot, my humble home;
There I was born, and when this life is o'er
I hope to sleep upon the river's shore.
There is the orchard which I helped to rear,
It well repays my labor year by year:
One apple tree towers high above the rest
Where every spring a blackbird has its nest.
Sweet Lily used to stand beneath the bough
And smiling listen—but she comes not now.
A fairer bird ne'er charmed the rising day
Than she we loved thus early called away;
But she is gone to sing her holy strains
In lovelier gardens and on greener plains.

There are the fields that I myself have cleared
Of trees and brush, and where a waste appeared

The corn just ready for the sickle stands,
And golden pumpkins dot my fertile lands.
There are the pastures where my cattle feed,
My gentle kine supply the milk we need;
Sweet cream and cheese are daily on our board,
And clothing warm my snowy sheep afford.
There are the flowers my Annie loves to tend,—
How often do I see her smiling bend
To pluck the weeds, or teach the graceful vine
Around the string or slender pole to twine.
How often when the toils of day are done,
And I return just at the set of sun,
She comes to meet me down the verdant lane—
Sweet partner of my pleasures and my pain—
With snow-white buds amid her sunny hair,
To win my favor all her joy and care.
How often does she wander forth with me
And share my seat beneath the maple tree,
And smile and blush to hear my ardent lays
Recount her virtues and pour forth her praise.

Hark! 'tis her voice, sweet as the wildbird's song;
She comes to tell me I have tarried long:
I hear her now an old love ditty hum,
And now she calls—I come, dear love, I come.

THE RETURN.

Grateful to our sleepless eyes,
Lo, the beams of morn arise,
And the mountain-tops are gray
With the light of coming day,—
And the birds are on the wing.
With the happy birds we'll sing

Bidding doubt and gloom be gone,
Like the shadows at the dawn.

Yes, for eyes as bright as day
Glance adown the shady way;
Gentle voices with delight
Whisper, "They will come to-night";
Hearts as fond and true as ours
Wait for us in lovely bowers:
Nor shall wait for us in vain,
Faithful ones, we come again.

Where the bending willows weep,
And the mosses slowly creep,
We our harps neglected hung.
Soon again they will be strung,—
Forest, dell, and mountain stream
Will take up the blissful theme
When no longer doomed to roam
We can chant the praise of home.

Lo, in yonder sky the sun
Half his daily task has done;
We will rest beside the spring,
While the bird with folded wing
Sits within his cool retreat,
Shaded from the noontide heat,
And the bees, with drowsy hum,
Homeward, honey-laden come.

Homeward too our way we hold,
Laden, not with paltry gold,
But with treasures better far
Than the richest jewels are:
Simple, trusting hearts, content
With the blessings Heaven has lent.

Once within our love-lit cot,
Rich and great we envy not.

Lo, the shadows lengthen fast;
Now the well-known hills are past;
Now the forest, dark and tall—
Oh, how we remember all!
Now the pastures strewn with rocks,
Where we used to watch our flocks,—
Farther down the winding road,
See! it is our own abode.

Where the slanting sunbeams fall
On the lowly cottage wall,
Fancy can already trace
Each belov'd, familiar face:
One by one each form appears
Till our eyes are dim with tears;
If the foretaste be so sweet
Soon our joy will be complete!

Here we are! But all is still
Save the ever-murmuring rill,—
Save the hooting of the owl,
And the village watch-dog's howl.
Slowly swings the cottage door—
Shall we cross the threshold o'er?
Empty and deserted all—
Echo answers to our call!

Where the bending willow tree
Oft has sheltered thee and me,
Lo, the turf has been uptorn:
We have come,—but come to mourn!
Eyes are dim and lips are cold,
And our arms we sadly fold

Over hearts, till hushed and dead,
Never to be comforted!

No; our hearts shall still be strong,
For the journey is not long;
In a holy, deathless land
We shall meet our household band:
In the fairer bowers above,
They await the friends they love,
Oh, what joy with them to dwell,
Never more to say farewell!

THE OLD SUGAR CAMP.

[Whoever has attended a "sugaring off" in the woods will enjoy the reading of this poem—the description is so life-like and exhilarating. It is a home scene.]

Come let us away to the old Sugar Camp;
The sky is serene though the ground may be damp,—
And the little bright streams, as they frolic and run,
Turn a look full of thanks to the ice-melting sun;
While the warm southern winds, wherever they go,
Leave patches of brown 'mid the glittering snow.

The oxen are ready, and Carlo and Tray
Are watching us, ready to be on the way,
While a group of gay children, with platter and spoon,
And faces as bright as the roses of June,
O'er fences and ditches exultingly spring,
Light-hearted and careless as birds on the wing.

Where's Edwin? Oh, here he comes, loading his gun;
Look out for the partridges—hush! there is one!
Poor victim! a bang and a flutter—'tis o'er,—

And those fair dappled wings shall expand nevermore;
It was shot for our invalid sister at home,
Yet we sigh as beneath the tall branches we roam.

Our cheeks all aglow with the long morning tramp,
We soon come in sight of the old Sugar Camp;
The syrup already is placed in the pan,
And we gather around it as many as can,—
We try it on snow; when we find it is done
We fill up a mold for a dear absent one.

Oh, gayest and best of all parties are these,
That meet in the Camp 'neath the old maple trees,
Renewing the love and the friendship of years,—
They are scenes to be thought of with smiles and
    with tears
When age shall have furrowed each beautiful cheek,
And left in dark tresses a silvery streak.

Here brothers and sisters and lovers have met,
And cousins and friends we can never forget;
The prairie, the ocean, divide us from some,
Yet oft as the seasons for sugaring come,
The cup of bright syrup to friendship we'll drain,
And gather them home to our bosom again.

Dear Maple, that yieldeth a nectar so rare,
So useful in spring, and in summer so fair,—
Of autumn acknowledged the glory and queen,
Attendant on every Canadian scene,
Enshrined in our homes it is meet thou shouldst be
Of our country the emblem, O beautiful Tree!

TO A RABBIT.

Go to the green wood, go
   I oft shall sigh for thee,—
And yet rejoice to know,
   That thou art sporting free.

Go to the meadows green,
   Where summer holds her reign;
When winter spoils the scene
   Wilt thou return again?

A shelter thou wouldst find
   From every howling storm;
The heart thou leav'st behind
   Would still be true and warm.

Why dost thou struggle thus?
   Does every balmy breeze
That softly fanneth us,
   Tell of the waving trees?

Do yonder happy birds
   That sing for thee and me,
For chorus have the words
   So precious—" I am free?"

Go then, as free as they,
   As light and happy roam
With thy companions gay,
   Safe in thy forest home.

There—thou art gone; farewell!
   My heart leaps up with thine;
And I rejoice to tell
   Thou art no longer mine.

I could not breathe the air
　Where pining captives dwell;
My freedom thou wilt share,
　With joy then, fare-thee-well.

THE OLD MAN.

The old man's cheek was wet with tears,
　And his wrinkled brow was pale,
As after a lapse of many years
　He stood in his native vale.

The warblers sang in the leafy bough,
　And the earth was robed in green;
But the old man's heart beat sadly now
　While he gazed on the lovely scene.

The stream ran clear to the distant sea,
　The same as he saw it last;
And sitting beneath an old elm tree,
　He thought of days in the past.

He thought how he climbed the verdant hill,
　Or roved through the forest wild,
Or traced to its source the rippling rill,
　A gay and careless child.

And as he thought of the happy throng
　That around him used to crowd
With the ringing laugh and the joyous song,
　The old man wept aloud.

For well he knew they would meet no more
　On the dreary shores of time,—
But he looked away to a brighter shore,
　He looked to a deathless clime.

That moment a young and merry group
    Came bounding across the lea,
With rosy cheek, with ball and with hoop
    They came to the old elm tree.

They paused awhile in their noisy play
    To gaze on the aged man,
While he wiped his falling tears away
    And in trembling tones began :

" I would not cloud for the world your joy,
    Or have you less happy for me—
For I have been like yourselves a boy
    Though I'm now the wreck you see.

" But let the words of wisdom and truth
    In your memories be enrolled,—
And in the days of your sunny youth
    Be kind to the poor and old ! "

The children wept as they heard him speak,
    And forgetful of their play
They wiped the tears from his furrowed cheek,
    And they smoothed his locks of gray.

He laid his hand with a tender air
    By turns on each youthful head,
Then lifting his faded eyes in prayer,
    " God bless you ! " the old man said.

And the boys *were blest :*—for the angels flung
    Around them their wings of gold ;
So ever they do when the gay and young
    Are kind to the poor and old.

THE FADING AND THE UNFADING.

Once more the beautiful Spring has returned, and from my window I can behold the delightful places where I have so often roamed in childhood light-hearted and happy. But the lovely Spring brings no longer the same emotions as of yore. Oh no! for "a change has come over the spirit of my dream." Earth has lost its charms, and although I love the beauties of nature even better than before, still they cannot satisfy,—they are doomed to fade, and my soul yearns for those beautiful heavenly bowers which shall never wither; where God himself reigns in person and "chases night away." But, although I sigh for such things, am I prepared for them? Should I be ready at this moment to enter the paradise of God? Ah, my heart, why shouldest thou hesitate thus to return an answer? God is still able and willing to save, and though I have wandered so far from Him, if with an humble and penitent soul I confess my sins he is willing and able to forgive me.—*June 4, 1853.*

ON RECEIPT OF SOME WILD FLOWERS.

I bedewed with tears those spring-time flowers,
For they brought to my mind the happy hours
When I roamed through the forests and meadows green
With a heart all alive to each beautiful scene.

I loved the flowers when my step was light,
And my cheek with the glow of health was bright,

Through forest and meadows, o'er plain and o'er hill
I may wander no more—but I love them still!

I love the flowers, and I love them best
When they first peep out from earth's snow-wreathed
  breast;
For they tell, amid sorrow, and death, and gloom,
Of a spring that shall visit the depths of the tomb!

And oh! could I roam through Fortune's bowers,
I would twine a wreath of the sweetest flowers,
Whose beauty and fragrance should ne'er depart—
But brighten thy home and gladden thy heart!

But the flowers of earth are fragile and fair,—
And the young brow must fade and be furrowed with
  care;
But hast thou not heard of a wonderful clime
That ne'er has been marred by the footsteps of Time?

There in gardens of bliss the weary repose;
There the pale, sickly cheek wears the hue of the
  rose;
There death never comes,—Oh, amid its bright bowers,
May we twine for each other a garland of flowers!

THE SICK GIRL'S DREAM.

I heard the other night in dreams
  The early robin sing:
The southern winds unlocked the streams,
  And warmed the heart of Spring.

The plum-trees wore their bridal dress,
  The willows donned their plumes,

And to the zephyr's fond caress
　　Gave forth their rare perfumes.

Through months of wintry frost and storm—
　　Yet never harmed by them—
A million germs had nestled warm,
　　Close to the parent stem.

The happy spring-time broke their rest,
　　They drank the morning dew,
They clasped the sunbeams to their breast,
　　And clothed the trees anew.

The clouds distilled the fertile rain
　　And sent it forth in showers;
The sunlight danced along the plain
　　And painted it with flowers.

The butterfly went forth to play,
　　The useful honey bee
Kept up a hum through all the day
　　Of cheerful industry.

The squirrel gamboled in the grove,
　　The rabbit bounded by,
The wary spider spun and wove,
　　And trapped the careless fly.

From out the joyous, vocal wood
　　The song of warblers came:
The cuckoo, in a merry mood,
　　Told and re-told its name.

And when behind the purple hill
　　The sun went out of sight,
The frogs began with hearty will
　　Their concert for the night.

Such scenes had made, in brighter years.
  My heart with transport leap,
But now they touched the spring of tears,—
  I sobbed aloud in sleep.

And is there not some balm, I cried,
  'Mid nature's boundless wealth?
"Behold"—a gentle voice replied—
  "Behold the Fount of health!"

Just then a torrent met my eye,
  Fresh from the rock it burst;
I could have drained the fountain dry,
  So raging was my thirst.

Such deep emotions filled my soul
  I woke—the vision fled:
The moonbeams through the curtain stole,
  Ah! 'twas a dream, I said.

But well I know there is a land
  Where flows the living stream;
And when upon its banks I stand,
  Oh, then 'twill be no dream.

THE LAST SONG.

"Earth is fair, oh so fair,"—
  Sang a little, happy bird;
Though a prey to grief and care,
  With a smile I heard.
Sing again that blithesome strain,
  Precious little bird, I said;
For the heart that throbbed with pain
  Thou hast comforted!

"Earth is fair, oh so fair,"
  Louder sang the happy bird;
"What have I to do with care,
  Or with hope deferred?"
All the western sky was red
  With the beams of setting sun,
As the sportsman homeward sped
  With the fatal gun.

"Earth is fair, oh so fair,
  And I love the green earth well,"—
Death was in the balmy air,
  And the warbler fell!
Earth *is* fair—but earth no more
  Wears its pleasant green for thee,—
Cold and stiff and bathed in gore
  Underneath the tree.

Earth is fair, but alas!
  It hath many scenes of woe;
Happy they who through them pass,
  Sweetly singing as they go,—
Comforting some lonely heart,
  Making some weak spirit strong;—
So may I, and then depart,
  On my lips a song!

AN EVENING SCENE.

How still and calm! what fairer scene e'er met
The eye of mortal short of Paradise?
The quiet lake is like a mirror set
In richest green where sunset loves to see
Itself arrayed in crimson, pink and gold.
And e'en the proud old mountain bows his head

Shaggy with hemlocks, and appears well pleased
To view so grand a form reflected there.
Hark! o'er the polished surface how the loons
Call to each other, waking echoes wild
From crag and cliff, and waking in my heart
Sweet memories of other days and years
When health was on my cheek, and hope and love
O'er all the future wove one iris bright.
Ah, little prophets, do you then predict
A rainy morrow? By yon crimson west
I doubt your warnings; so in truth it seems
Does yonder farmer who, with shouldered scythe
From meadows fragrant with the new-mown hay,
Goes whistling homeward, glad to seek repose
Until another sun shall call him forth,
To gather into barns the winter's store
Of food provided for the gentle kine
That faintly lowing from the pastures come
Scented with herbage, giving promise fair
Of pails o'erflowing with a sweeter drink
Than ever gleamed in the inebriate's bowl.

Now o'er the landscape signs of twilight creep,
And sounds that tell of night—sounds that I love:
The hooting of the owl, the tree-frog's cry
By distance mellowed; and—more distant still—
I hear the barking of the village dogs.
The breath of evening whispering 'mid the pines,
And deepening shadows, bid me homeward turn;
And yet I linger—for I seem a part
Of lake and mountain, meadow, tree and sky,—
And realize how sweet a thing it is
To lay my heart so close to Nature's own
That I can feel its throbbing, while each pulse
Responsive beats, and o'er my being steals
A rapturous calm like that our parents felt

When to the bowers of Eden they repaired,
And praised their Maker seen in all his works.

Author of nature! Source of life and light!
Almighty Father! let me praise thee too.
This lovely world is thine; yon moon and stars
That now begin to usher in the night
Are but the outposts of unnumbered spheres
That march in order round thy dazzling throne,
And chant thy praises in perpetual song.
All these are thine, for thou hast made them all;
And I am thine! I thank thee, Lord of lords,
King of the Universe, Creator, God,
That while in part I realize thy *power*
I know it has an equal in the *love*
Which bowed the heavens and consecrated earth
When the Messiah came to save mankind,
And in its proper orbit reinstate
A fallen world, which shall one day become
The fairest 'mid the sisterhood of orbs,
The most renowned because the dearest bought,—
The best beloved, because the ransom given
Was all that God omnipotent could pay!

AUTUMN TEACHINGS.

The howling winds rage around my casement. The summer is past, and everything indicates that winter will soon be here. The seared leaves are falling from their homes in the waving forests; the earth has thrown aside her gay mantle of green, and one scene of desolation presents itself to the eye. The decay of nature brings with it sad and solemn reflections, how much more the decay of the human form—of which autumn seems so striking an emblem. The days of man are few. Like the flower of the field he perisheth, and yet how few seem to realize it! O God, teach me to apply my heart unto wisdom. Help me to love and serve thee, that when "the heavens shall be dissolved and the elements shall melt with fervent heat" I may not be among those who shall take up the sad lamentation: "The harvest is past, the summer is ended, and we are not saved."—*Oct.*, 1852.

THE WATCHER.

[As Miss Johnson lived in the house with Dr. G. O. Somers, who would frequently in winter cross lake Memphremagog on the ice in visiting his patients, the following, written on a sick-bed, gives a graphic description of what her fears pictured might be a reality.]

Night comes, but he comes not! I fear
The treacherous ice; what do I hear?
Bells? nay, I am deceived again,—
'Tis but the ringing in my brain.
Oh how the wind goes shrieking past!
Was it a voice upon the blast?
A cry for aid? My God protect!
Preserve his life—his course direct!
How suddenly it has grown dark—
How very dark without—hush! hark!
'Tis but the creaking of the door;
It opens wide, and nothing more.
Then wind and snow came in; I thought
Some straggler food and shelter sought;

But more I feared, for fear is weak,
That some one came of him to speak:
To tell how long he braved the storm,
How long he kept his bosom warm
With thoughts of home, how long he cheered
His weary horse that plunged, and reared,
And wallowed through the drifted snow
Till daylight faded, and the glow
Of hope went out; how almost blind,
He peered around, below, behind,—
No road, no track, the very shore
All blotted out,—one struggle more,
It is thy last, perchance, brave heart!
O God! a reef! the masses part
Of snow and ice, and dark and deep
The waters lie in death-like sleep;
He sees too late the chasm yawn;
Sleigh, horse and driver, all are gone!
Father in heaven! It may be thus,
But thou art gracious,—pity us,
Save him, and me in mercy spare
What 'twould be worse than death to bear.
Hark! hark! am I deceived again?
Nay, 'tis no ringing in my brain;
My pulses leap—my bosom swells—
Thank God! it is, *it is his bells!*

Patriotic Poems.

THE SURRENDER OF QUEBEC.

[Quebec is the oldest city in Canada, having been founded by Champlain, in 1608, near the site of an Indian village. It was taken from the French, by the English, under General Wolfe, in 1759, after a heroic defence by Montcalm. Both generals fell on the battle-field, mortally wounded. In 1853 the Literary and Historical Society of Quebec offered a prize medal for the best poem relating to the history of Canada. Miss JOHNSON (then in her eighteenth year) wrote the following, which took the prize.]

The orb of day upon his pathway pressed,
Beaming with splendor, toward the shining west,
Cast one long, lingering glance upon the scene,
Lit up the river and the forest green,
Left his last rays upon the lordly dome,
And deigned to smile upon the peasant's home;
Then 'neath the western hills he sought repose,
And sank to rest as calmly as he rose:
Bright at the dawn of day, but brighter now,
When day had almost passed, and round her brow
Hung the expiring beams of dazzling light,
The certain presage of approaching night.
Slowly his gorgeous train, like him, withdrew,
Changing as they advanced in form and hue,
Until one lovely tint of fairest dye
Stole softly o'er the calm and cloudless sky;
Day, gently smiling, left her gleaming throne,
And evening fair came forth, and reigned alone.
The twinkling stars the azure vault adorned;

Like glistening gems, a glorious crown they formed,
And proudly sat in splendor pure and bright
Upon the pale and pensive brow of night;
While in the midst of all, with tranquil mein,
Mild Cynthia lent enchantment to the scene.

Beneath lay spreading pastures green and fair,
And lofty hills and waving forests, where
The human voice had never yet been heard,
Or other sound, save when the depths were stirred
By the loud screams of some lone midnight bird.
But high o'er all the lofty city rose,
Firm in its strength, sublime in its repose;
On every hand by nature fortified,
And strongly built; with air of conscious pride
Gazed from its heights upon the scene below,
And bade defiance to each lurking foe;
Confiding in its bulwarks firm and sure,
It calmly slept and deemed itself secure!

The river swept along; with surging roar
Its waves dashed wildly on the rocky shore;
While on its broad, expansive bosom lay
The twinkling orbs in beautiful array;
And every pearly drop shone clear and bright,
Bathed in a flood of soft and silvery light.
Scarcely a ripple stirred its quiet breast;
For every sighing breeze was lulled to rest,
And every sound was hushed on earth, in air,
And silence held supreme dominion there.

Sleep sent his angels forth; with silent tread,
From house to house, they on their mission sped;
Watched by the couch of suffering and pain.
Soothed the pale brow and calmed the throbbing brain,
Eased the sad heart and closed the weeping eye,

Bade care and grief with their attendants fly,
Entered the chamber of the rich and great,
Nor scorned to visit those of mean estate,
But blessed alike the lofty and the low,
Alike bade each forget their weight of woe.
The proud and wealthy drew around their breast
"The curtains of repose," and sank to rest;
The pallid sons of want and hunger slept,
And sorrow's sons forgot that they had wept.

   The night wore slowly on; the dismal tower
Had long since tolled the lonely midnight hour
When a proud band, by daring impulse led,
Approached the river with a cautious tread,
With kindling eye and with an eager air,
Unmoored the boats that waited for them there;
In silence left the calm and peaceful shore,
In sullen silence plied the hasty oar,
In silence passed adown the quiet stream,
While ever and anon a pale moonbeam,
Sad and reproachful, cast a hasty glance
On polished dagger and on gleaming lance.

   The scene was mournful, and with magic art
It acted strangely on each manly heart;
No speedy action now, no rude alarm,
Called forth their powers, or nerved the stalwart arm;
No present danger used its strong control,
To rouse the passions of the warrior's soul;
But all conspired to place Thought on her throne,
And yield the reins of power to her alone.

   The past came slowly forth with all its train
Of blissful scenes that ne'er might be again,
Of mournful partings and convulsive sighs,
Of pallid faces and of tearful eyes,

Of aching hearts that heaved with sorrow's swell,
And broken tones that sadly breathed, "Farewell!"
And in the silence of that lonely hour,
Which bade the sternest own its wondrous power,
A small, still voice whispered in every soul,
Although each sought to burst from its control:
" To-morrow night the moon, as fair as now,
May shed her beams upon your death-sealed brow!
To-morrow night the stars may gild the wave
While you, perchance, may fill a soldier's grave!
To-morrow night your spirit may explore
The boundless regions of an unknown shore!
To-morrow night may find you with the slain,
And weeping love watch your return in vain!"

And yet not long such gloomy thoughts might rest
Within the soldier's brave and gallant breast;
Not long the warrior, panting for the field
And for the battle's horrid din, might yield
His fearless spirit unto sorrow's sway,
Or dread the issue of the coming day.
The momentary sadness now was o'er,
As with new hopes they neared the frowning shore,
Landed in silence, and in stern array
Pressed firmly forward on their dangerous way,
Mounted the rugged rocks with footsteps slow,
And left the murmuring river far below.

From cliff to cliff the gallant army spring,
Nor envy now the eagle's soaring wing;
They view their labors o'er, their object gain,
And proudly stand upon the lovely plain;
Gaze down upon the awful scenes they've passed,
Rejoicing that they've reached the heights at last.
Hope lights each eye and fills each manly breast,
Where wild desires and aspirations rest;

It bids each doubt and every shadow flee,
And points them on to certain victory!

The morning dawned; the orient beams of light
Fell on a strange and a romantic sight,—
On glistening helmet and on nodding crest,
On waving banner and on steel-clad breast.
The city woke,—but woke to hear the cry,
" To arms! to arms! the foe—the foe is nigh!"
She woke to hear the trumpet's wild alarms—
She woke to hear the sound of clashing arms—
She woke to view her confidence removed—
She woke to view her trusted safety proved;
Her mighty bulwarks, long her pride and boast,
All safely mounted by a British host—
She woke to view her lofty ramparts yield,
Her plains converted to a battle-field,
Her gallant troops in wild disorder fly,
The British banner floating to the sky,
And proudly waving o'er the bloody plain,
O'er heaps of dying and o'er heaps of slain.

Roused from their hasty dreams, with brows aghast,
On every hand the soldiers gather fast,
Bind on their armor, seize the glittering sword,
Form in a line, and at a simple word,
With hurried steps advance toward the shore,
With hasty gestures grasp the trembling oar,
Across the river's bosom swiftly glide
And safely land upon the other side.
Drawn up in battle order now they stand,
Waiting in silence for their chief's command;
Then onward move, with firm and stately tread,
With waving plumes and ensigns proudly spread,
With gleaming sword and with uplifted lance,
Where brightly now the glistening sunbeams dance;

But long before those sunbeams shall decline
Streams of dark blood shall tarnish all their shine;
Those beams shall strive to gild the steel in vain,
For human gore the polished steel shall stain.

The sun rose clear that morn; with ardent glow
He shed his beams alike o'er friend and foe.
His golden hues the spreading fields adorn,
Waving in beauty with the ripening corn;
Give richer colors to the lofty trees,
That gently rustle in the morning breeze;
They gild the river's surface, calm and blue,
And shine reflected in the sparkling dew.

Oh, ye, who stand prepared for deadly strife,
Thirsting for blood and for a brother's life,
Behold the glories that around you lie,
The harmony pervading earth and sky!
Behold the wondrous skill and power displayed
In every leaf and every lowly blade;
On every hand behold the wondrous love
Of Him who reigns in majesty above,—
Who bids for man all nature sweetly smile,
And sends his rain upon the just and vile;
His attribute is love; and shall ye dare
To take the life mercy and love would spare?
Shall ye destroy what he has formed to live,
And take away what ye can never give?
Shall puny mortal claim the right his own
Belonging to Omnipotence alone?
Rash man, forbear! and stay the ready dart
That seeks to lodge within thy brother's heart.
But, no; for mercy's voice, now hushed and still,
No longer may the steel-clad bosom thrill;
And hearts that melted once at other's woe—
That kindled once with friendship's fervent glow—

That once had felt and owned the soothing power
Of tender love—are callous in the hour
When savage War makes bare his awful arm
And peals in thunder tones his dread alarm.

But there were *some* in those devoted bands
O'er whom the blissful scenes of other lands
Came rushing wildly; and with piercing gaze
They looked an instant on their boyhood's days;
Remembered well the hours that flew too fast,
Remembered *some* with whom those hours were past;
And, 'mid the group of dear companions gay,
Remembered well some whom they saw that day;
But sprang not forward with familiar grasp
And friendly air, the proffered hand to clasp;
But looked away, and with a pang of pain
Regretted that they e'er had met again!
For now they met, not as they met before—
Not as they used to meet in days of yore;
Not arm in arm, like brothers fondly tried,
Whom they could trust and in whose love confide;
Met not as once with high and mutual aim,
In classic halls to seek for future fame:
But met as bitter foes, in deadly strife,
Each wildly panting for the other's life;
With armies proud and swelling like the flood,
To wreath their laurels in each other's blood!

They once were friends; but France and England rose
In sounding arms and they are hostile foes!
They once were friends; but friendship may not shield
The warrior's breast upon the battle-field!
They once were friends; but, hark! the cannon's roar
Loudly proclaims that they are friends no more!
From rank to rank the stunning volley flies,

From rank to rank the groans of anguish rise ;
Rank after rank is numbered with the slain ;
Rank follows rank, and bleeds upon the plain.

Bravely they fought ; with unabated zeal
In human gore they dipped the shining steel ;
Pressed o'er the heaps of dying and of dead,
Where warriors groaned, and gallant heroes bled ;
While from their lips, in quick and stifled breath
Arose the cry of " Victory, or death."

Louder and louder still the awful roar
Pealed from the heights, and shook the frightened shore.
Thick clouds of smoke enveloped friend and foe ;
The volleyed thunder shook the depths below ;
Mountain and echoing forest joined the cry,
And distant hills gave back the same reply.
With animating voice and waving hand
The British leader cheered his gallant band.
Pressed firmly forward where one endless tide
Of woe and carnage reigned on every side,—
Where streams of blood in crimson torrents rolled,—
Where death smote down alike the young and old ;
And where the thickest poured the deadly shot,
The gallant WOLFE with daring valor fought.

The dead and dying in his pathway lie,
Before him ranks divide and squadrons fly ;
With stalwart arm, and with unerring aim,
He adds new glories to his former fame,
Reaps the reward of all his toil : for now
Fresh laurels twine around his youthful brow.
But what avail they ? for the fatal dart
Of death has lodged within that hoping heart !
The lofty head that wore the waving crest,

Now sadly droops upon the bleeding breast;
That mighty arm, upraised in power and pride,
Falls feebly down, and casts its sword aside;
The laurel wreath entwines that brow in vain,
For, lo! the hero lies among the slain!

    The French fought long with courage and with skill;
With iron arms and with an iron will
Rushed bravely forward 'mid the battle's din,
Resolved to die, or else the victory win;
Like soldiers true, fought firmly and fought well,
And at their post like faithful soldiers fell.

    Deeper and deeper now the conflict grows;
Despair nerves these, and victory flushes those.
'Tis the last struggle; hark! "They fly! they fly!"
Pierces the depths, and rends the vaulted sky.
'Tis the last struggle, for the beating drum
Proclaims the conflict o'er, the victory won.
The French in wild dismay and horror yield,
And leave the British masters of the field.

    Far in the rear a dying warrior lay,
While from his breast the life-blood ebbed away;
Attendants bent around to staunch the tide
That flowed in torrents from his wounded side;
With wild convulsions came each panting breath,
And those proud features wore the hue of death.
His lips were sealed, his beaming eyes were dim,
And strangely quivered every outstretched limb;
Unconscious now he seemed of love or hate,
Unconscious now his spirit seemed to wait
The awful summons that should bid it fly
To worlds unknown, unseen by human eye.
He seemed like one already with the dead;

When, lo! he started—raised his drooping head;
With dying hand he grasped his trusty blade,
With kindling eye the battle-field surveyed,
Heard the triumphant shout, "They run! they run!"
Knew that the field was gained, the victory won.
"Who run?" he cried, with wildly throbbing heart,
With gushing breast, and livid lips apart.
"The French! the French!"—no more that warrior
 heard;
It was enough for him, that single word;
"I die contented!" and his youthful head
Fell feebly back; the noble soul had fled.

Oh, gallant Wolfe! from o'er the dark blue sea
There comes a wail—a bitter wail for thee;
Thy country mourns her warrior, true and brave,
And yearning love weeps o'er thy lowly grave.
But nothing now may break thy tranquil rest,
Nothing disturb thy calm and quiet breast;
Nor clashing arms, nor cannon's deafening roar,
Nor sorrow's wail, may ever rouse thee more.
But, when a voice, far louder than them all,
Shall bid thee rise, thou must obey the call,
And stand, bereft of earthly pride and power,
Before thy Judge. God shield thee in that hour!

Remoter from the scene, with drooping head
And nerveless arm, another warrior bled!
Death's seal upon that pallid brow was pressed;
His icy hand lay on that heaving breast;
But thoughts of victory lent no soothing balm
To cheer the spirit of the proud Montcalm!
He lived to see his bravest followers die;
He lived to see his troops disbanded fly;
Nor longer cared to live, but welcomed death,
And with a smile resigned his fleeting breath;

Stretched his proud limbs, without a sigh or groan,
And death had claimed the hero for his own.

The strife was o'er, the dreadful combat past;
The echoing hills had found repose at last;
Carnage had done its work on every side,
And even greedy death was satisfied!
The sun went down; how changed from yester night!
How changed his aspect, and how changed the sight
On which he gazed! Then his last golden beam
Fell on a landscape fair—a quiet scene—
Where now destruction reared its standard dread
O'er shattered bodies and o'er severed head.

Heap upon heap the pallid victims lay,
Of racking pain and scorching thirst the prey;
In anguish rolled upon the bloody ground,
And wider still they tore each gaping wound;
In concert joined their agonizing cries,
Gnashed with their teeth and rolled their blood-shot
    eyes;
With feeble groans they drew each painful breath,
And racked with torments called aloud for death!
Far o'er the field in wild confusion rose
Piles of the ghastly dead—of friends and foes—
In death stretched side by side, mangled and cold
While over all the sulphurous war-clouds rolled,
In dark, dense columns mounted up on high,
Tainting the air, polluting all the sky.

Quebec was won; and o'er each lofty tower
The British banner streamed in pride and power;
Where the French eagle once her wings had spread
The British lion reared his haughty head,
And shook the conquered country with his roar;
The eagle flew in terror from the shore.

With drooping plumage skimmed the western main,
And, trembling, sought her native France again;
While England, proud and potent, took the sway
And waved her sceptre over Canada.

SONG OF THE ENGLISH PEASANT GIRL.

[The marriage in 1858 of Prince Frederick William of Prussia to Victoria Adelaide Mary, eldest daughter of the Queen of England ; and the visit of Albert Edward, Prince of Wales, to Canada, in 1860, were events of sufficient magnitude to arouse the patriotism of our Canadian poetess, and we find reference made to them in this and the two following pieces.]

I am but a rustic maiden
    Dwelling by the river side,
But I'm happy as the Princess
    Who today becomes a bride.

I am but a peasant's daughter,
    All his life in toil is spent,
But he loves me as Prince Albert
    Loves his child, and I'm content.

Though the Queen of many nations,
    Centre of each Royal scene,
Better than I love my mother,
    Does the Princess love the Queen ?

Are Prince Leopold and Arthur,
    Though within a palace bred,
Dearer than my little brothers
    Playing 'neath the cottage shed ?

There's a group of Royal sisters
    Clustering round the English throne,

But I know they are not truer,
   Better sisters than mine own.

Hark! it is the trumpet sounding;
   At the Prince of Prussia's side
Standeth now her Royal Highness;
   Oh, I would not be the bride!

For a manly voice hath whispered,
   "Dearer than my life thou art!"
What care I who rules a kingdom
   If I rule in Jamie's heart?

I am but a peasant's daughter,
   And the wealthy pass me by,—
But there's not in merry England
   A happier maid than I.

A NATION'S DESIRE.

God hear our fervent prayer,
God bless the royal pair,
   God save the Queen!
Guide them in all their ways,
And may their wedded days
Be ordered to thy praise;
   God save the Queen!

The waves will soon divide
Thee and thy home, young bride;
   God save the Queen!
But over land and sea
Warm hearts will follow thee,
First rose of England's tree;
   God save the Queen.

CANADA'S WELCOME.

A nation's hearty welcome take,
   Heir to a mighty throne;
Thrice welcome! for old England's sake,
   Thy mother's, and thine own.

From crowded street, from hillside green,
   From fair Canadian vales,
The prayer goes up—God bless the Queen!
   God bless the Prince of Wales!

The rich and poor, the great and small
   Their voices join as one;
Victoria's name is dear to all,
   So is Victoria's Son.

Their tribute other queens have laid
   Upon the land and sea;
But never earthly monarch swayed
   So many hearts as she.

And for her young and gallant heir
   A kindred love prevails;
God hear a nation's fervent prayer!
   God bless the Prince of Wales!

OUR NATIVE LAND.

[This was probably written in the early part of the year 1861, before Lincoln's Emancipation Proclamation had given deliverance to the captives, and when "the north star" was an object dear to many a slave who longed to breathe the free air of Canada. The Rev. E. H. Dewart says of it: "This spirited lyric is alike creditable to the talents, patriotism, and independence of its author. Its loyalty is an intelligent attainment, free from blind prejudice and crouching adulation."

What land more beautiful than ours?
  What other land more blest?
The South with all its wealth of flowers?
  The prairies of the West?

Oh no! there's not a fairer land
  Beneath yon azure dome—
Where Peace holds Plenty by the hand,
  And Freedom finds a home.

The slave who but her name hath heard,
  Repeats it day and night,
And envies every little bird
  That takes its northward flight.

As to the Polar star they turn
  Who brave a pathless sea:
So the oppressed in secret yearn,
  Dear native land, for thee!

How many loving memories throng
  Round Britain's stormy coast!
Renowned in story and in song,
  Her glory is our boast.

With loyal hearts we still abide
  Beneath her sheltering wing,—
While with true patriot love and pride,
  To Canada we cling.

We wear no haughty tyrant's chain,—
  We bend no servile knee,
When to the Mistress of the main
  We pledge our fealty.

She binds us with the cords of love,—
  All others we disown;

The rights we owe to God above,
    We yield to him alone.

May He our future course direct
    By his unerring hand;
Our laws and liberties protect,
    And bless our native land.

THE APPEAL.

[It will be remembered that 1861 closed with an alarming prospect of war between England and the United States, growing partly out of the arrest of Mason and Slidell on board the British steamship Trent. Of course had war been declared Canada would have been involved. On Christmas of that year therefore Miss JOHNSON wrote this appeal, which was published in a Canadian paper:]

To prayer! to prayer! O ye who love
    Your country's peace, your country's weal,
To Him who rules supreme above,
    In this dark hour of peril kneel.
To prayer! to prayer! before the cry
    "To arms!" shall make your spirit quake,—
And ere ye dream of danger nigh
    The dark portentous war-cloud break.

So long hath Peace o'er hill and vale
    Waved her white banner to the breeze,
We thought her smiles would never fail,
    And only heard from o'er the seas
The murmur of an angry host,
    The clang of arms, the cannon's roar,—
How false our hope! how vain our boast!
    War threatens our beloved shore.

Great God! to whom the nations seem
    Like dust that gathers on the scales,
A drop within a mighty stream,
    A breath amid the northern gales,
We pray, the hearts of men dispose
    So that the sounds of war may cease,
And nations who should ne'er be foes
    Embrace, and pledge themselves to Peace.

I LOVE THE LAND WHERE I WAS BORN.

[The following poem appeared in the *Sherbrooke* (*P. Q.*) *Gazette*, sometime in the winter of 1863, and was the last article prepared by Miss JOHNSON for the press. It is of special interest for having been written during the dark days of the war in the United States, and when the sympathy of England and Canada for the North was by many questioned.]

I love the land where I was born,
    'Tis a noble land and good;
It has many a field of wheat and corn
    Where once the forest stood;
It has many a town and city grand,
    Where the Savage used to roam;
To the poor of every other land
    It offers a peaceful home.

I'm proud of the land where I was born,
    I'm proud of the Parent Isle,
Whose banners float at the gates of morn,
    And the gates of eve the while.
And my pulses leap with a joyous thrill,
    Wherever they take the lead,
And join their hands with a hearty will
    In doing a noble deed.

There's another land that's dear to me,
  For it speaks the English tongue;
Like a shoot that springs from an old oak tree,
  From the English race it sprung.
It has gained a mighty place on earth,
  And a mighty name has won;
It has given to sage and hero birth,
  And it boasts of Washington.

But a blot, a dark and loathsome blot,
  Polluted that fair young land;
God waited till his wrath was hot,
  And he took his sword in hand!
He had heard the bitter wail of woe,
  He had heard the clanking chain—
He rescued a nation years ago,
  He will rescue one again!

There's a gathering darkness in the sky,
  There's a tramp of hurrying feet;
There's a clang of arms, and a battle cry,
  And two hostile armies meet.
They meet! they charge! 'tis a dreadful sight!
  They wade through a gory sea;
It is life or death, it is wrong or right,
  It is freedom or slavery!

The nations stand with a wondering look,
  And list to the roar and din;
While History bends o'er an open book
  And steadily writes therein.
And what will she say of my native land?
  And what of the Parent Isle?
To the North, or South, did they give their hand,
  To which did they grant a smile?

God speaks in the wind and earthquake now,
   And those who have ears may hear :
To the King of kings let monarchs bow,
   And let all the earth draw near.
Let the nations mark his holy laws,
   For though he keeps silence long,
With fire and sword He will plead the cause
   Of the weak against the strong.

Take heed and beware, my native land,—
   To thy ways and words take heed!
On the side of right and freedom stand,
   And say to the truth, "God speed!"
Let England herself a lesson learn,
   And let her take warning too;
Let her judge as she would be judged in turn,
   Let her nobly speak and do.

THE WORLD TO COME.

[Dear as Canada was to our authoress, dearer still to her heart was the true Father-Land, " the heavenly country " for which the children of faith in the olden time looked. Being born again she bore such a relationship to the world to come that we may say of her, as she does of " the bride of Christ ": " The Cross was infinitely dearer to her than ten thousand worlds. It was twined around her heart with ties that nothing could ever loose. She wept, but they were mingled tears of joy and sorrow: sorrow, for she mourned that her sins had cost the life of the Son of God; joy, for she knew that that sacrifice had made a perfect atonement for her. She knew that the Father had forgiven her iniquities, and that he would no longer remember her sins. As she clung to the Cross, a bright beam of glory shone around her; she raised her tearful eyes, and a crown of everlasting beauty met her admiring

gaze: she knew that crown was reserved for her, and that on her bridal day her Lord would place it on her own brow."
With such an experience and such a hope, we are not surprised that she should thus discourse:]

The earth renewed presents a glorious scene:
Mountains and valleys of perpetual green;
Delicious plains, and odoriferous bowers,
Unfading forests, never-dying flowers;
Fruits that on fragrant trees immortal grow,
Rivers that murmur sweetly as they flow,
And gardens decked with everlasting spring,
And shining warblers on the tireless wing.
No howling tempest breaks the sweet repose,
No piercing thorn surrounds the blushing rose,
No sultry heat parches those blooming plains,
No night is known where day forever reigns;
No thunder's roar, no lightning's vivid glare,
No darkened sky, disturbs the beauty there.

The royal city, the divine abode
Of ransomed men and their eternal God,
Rises 'mid blooming bowers and lofty trees,
And waves its banners to the gentle breeze.
Upon its pearly gates and shining walls
A flood of everlasting glory falls,
And tinges with its own delightful glow
The lovely river murmuring below.
That river from the living fountain springs,
And, guided by the mighty King of kings,
It wanders through the saints' celestial home,
Where, robed in white, the ransomed nations roam
Through golden streets, and gardens fair and free;
And on its banks stands life's unfading tree.
All, all is bliss, and love, and glory there;
No pain, no sickness, no corroding care,
No grief, no aching hearts, no tearful eyes,

No broken bands, and there no severed ties;
For, o'er those broad and beautiful domains
The Prince of peace, the great Immanuel reigns.
The good have met, of every age and land,
Around the throne a glorious throng they stand;
The crown of life, the blood-washed robes they wear,
The conqueror's palms of victory they bear;
They bend the knee, they raise the joyful eye;
And hark! Oh, hark! that vast assembly cry:
"Worthy the Lamb to be exalted thus,
Worthy the Lamb, for he was slain for us!"
And angels with the ransomed millions sing,
"Glory and honor to our God and King!"

Temperance.

A WELCOME TO A TEMPERANCE PICNIC.

Old and young are welcome here
   To the banquet we have spread:
It will cause no bitter tear
   When the festal hour is fled;
It will break no mother's heart,
   For the deadly bowl we shun!
Welcome then—and when we part
   Blessings go with every one.

[The following lines were also written by Miss JOHNSON for a temperance picnic, held in a grove near her father's house. They were read by her brother Edwin, now a lawyer in Stanstead, P. Q.]

From north and south, from east and west
   They come with banners gay;
Hope lights each eye and fills each breast,
   And all are friends to-day.

The fairest of the sister band—
   With greeting most sincere,—
Magog extends an eager hand,
   And bids you welcome here!

Hail, brothers in a noble cause,
   'Tis well we thus should meet:
For every meeting closer draws
   The bonds of union sweet.

And we who battle for the right,
    And breathe the solemn vow
To win or perish in the fight,
    Should be united now.

Up, brothers, up! to arms! to arms!
    The sword must needs be drawn:
These are indeed no vain alarms,
    The foe is marching on!

And shall he blight our happy land
    With his polluting breath?
And scatter woe on every hand,
    And infamy and death?

By yonder mountain and by lake
    Which their approval show,—
For each beloved Township's sake,
    We boldly answer—No!

Then let our banners be unfurled,
    'Mid scorn or 'mid applause;
We dare proclaim to all the world
    We love the temperance cause!

A LIFE-SCENE—THE LETTER.

"I'm at work upon the railroad"—
    So the brother's letter ran,—
"I'm at work upon the railroad,
    With the wages of a man.

"I am up at peep of morning,
    And I only stop to eat;
But I bear it all extremely well
    Except the noon-day heat.

"I do not feel much homesick,
    Though I think of other scenes,
And what you have for dinner
    When I eat my pork and beans!

" 'Tis the time for pies and dumplings,
    Currant jelly and all that,
For an hour in mother's pantry
    I'd give my bran-new hat.

" You wrote about the chickens,
    About the crops and hay;
But not a word about the colts—
    The black one or the gray.

" Tell father not to worry
    About that note at all:
I shall have a hundred dollars
    I can send him in the fall.

" You cannot think how proudly
    It makes my bosom swell,
To think that I am toiling
    For those I love so well.

" Tell mother I remember
    Her parting words to me;
And all that she has prayed for
    I hope I yet may be.

" The workmen bring the bottle,
    They say, 'Just take a sip;'
But, mother, *not a single drop
    Shall ever touch my lip.*

" Here's a kiss for brother Charley—
    The little roguish elf,

I hope he'll not forget me,—
And another for yourself.

"How much I want to see you
I will not try to tell;
I never knew I loved my home
And all my friends so well!

"My lamp is burning dimly,
So, sister dear, good-night;
Think often of your brother,
And don't forget to write."

The sister read the letter
With a look of pride and joy;
And the father and the mother said,
"God bless the darling boy!"

THE PLEDGE.

[Whether the following is a real or a supposed case we know that in this fallen world of ours there have been many sadder scenes than the one depicted; for "who hath woe? who hath sorrow? who hath contentions? who hath babbling? who hath wounds without cause? who hath redness of eyes? They that tarry long at the wine; they that go to seek mixed wine. . . . At the last it biteth like a serpent, and stingeth like an adder."—Prov. 23 : 29–35.]

PART I.

All day the snow came silently to earth,
Until the branches of the apple trees
Bent lower than in autumn 'neath their weight
Of glossy fruit: the youthful pines that stood,
With leafless beech and maple interspersed,

To speak of summer when all else that laughed
In balmy air with summer should depart,
Were robed in white, save where some little twig
Of deepest verdure timidly looked forth,
Like gentle Spring reclining in the arms
Of stern old Winter. Silence reigned abroad ;
There was no sun, no sky, but over all
A dense dark mist which hid the blue beyond.

The cottager had tarried long that day
Within the village inn, and night drew near
And found him at his glass ; then rose the wind
And hurled the snow against the window pane.
" Come, father, come " ; a little hand was laid
Upon the father's arm, and into his
A pair of pleading eyes looked gently up.
" Come, father, come ; the wind begins to blow,
And mother waits and watches all alone."
He heeded not the warning ; to the bar
He gaily turned, and cried, " Another glass ! "
The glass was drained, and yet another filled,—
And still the pleader cried, " Come, father, come."

" The night is cold," one thoughtless comrade said
" And you have far to walk ; here, drink, my boy.
The child pushed back the tempter's hand, a glow
Of indignation mantling cheek and brow,—
" My mother says there's poison in the cup,
And I will never drink," he firmly said.
The father gave him an approving smile,
Patted his rounded cheek, and stroked his curls,
Then heaved a sigh—while o'er his manly face,
Which had been handsome ere the fatal wine
Disfigured it, a mournful shadow crept
And darkened all his soul. " Come, father, come : "

This time he listened, clasped the little hand,
And they went forth together in the storm.

The wind blew fiercely from the north and east,
And called its forces from the neighboring hills;
They heard the summons, eager to obey,
And swept along in one continuous roar.
They caught the snow new-fallen from the earth
And wove a sheet with which to blind the eyes
Of those two wanderers on the frozen waste.
Then night came on; dark night came suddenly,
And hid within its bosom bush and tree,
And all that stood as waymarks to their home.
The little winding path they trod that morn
Was now a path no more; yet had his brain
Been clear as on the morn, his step as firm,
The father might have found his homeward way.
But oft the earth seemed reeling 'neath his feet,
And once he fell, then nerved himself anew
To struggle with the storm.

                  "How long the way!
Dear father, are we almost home at last?"
Through teeth that chattered came the words half-
    formed,
And drops of dew stole from his anxious eyes
And turned to pearly ice-drops where they fell.
And then the father took the patient boy
Within his arms; he hugged him to his breast
And tried with steady gaze to pierce the gloom
If he might catch a glimpse of friendly lights,
Or haply of the lamp that burned for him
In his own cottage, fed by one who watched,
And wept, and prayed, and turned the cottage door
Upon its frosty hinges, till her fair cheek
Grew purple with the cold; he thought of this,

And anguish and remorse smote heavily.
But deeper grew the night; and hours that seemed
Like years to that distracted father passed.
Nearer and nearer to his aching breast
He held the child—for hope grew faint within;
Yet with that precious burden at his heart
He could not quite despair. "If I have sinned,
If I am seen in Heaven's all-searching light
Black and polluted, yet my child is pure,
And for the father's sin he should not die.
Guard him, ye angels! Save him, O my God!"
Thus in the depths of his own soul he prayed,
And chafed again the little trembling hands,
And kissed the cheek so cold it spoke of death.

"Let me kneel down, dear father; let me pray,
For I am weary—I will sleep awhile;
But ere I sleep, dear father, let me pray."
And round his father's neck he twined his arms,
And faintly whispered half his evening prayer.
O wretched father! O polluted man!
Is it the wind that makes thee shiver thus?

Part II.

All day the snow came silently to earth,
Until the path before the cottage door
Was even with the drift on either side.
No foot disturbed the mass of crystals white,
But when the wind began to roar and shriek,
And Night descended, with her sable wing
Darkening the scene around, a pallid face
Which had been pressed against the window pane
For half an hour, came forth into the gloom.
As looks the moon upon some stormy night
When every star is quenched, and she alone
Through rifted clouds peers forth and keeps her watch:

So looked that wife and mother as she stood
Upon the threshold gazing down the road
With chattering teeth, and limbs that quaked with
　　cold,
Imagining she heard in every gust
The voice and footfall of the man she loved.

The hearth was piled with blazing logs that shed
A cheerful glow upon the cottage walls;
The table spread for three before it stood,
And yet the bread was all unbroken there,—
And from the cottage to the garden gate
A shivering form went flitting to and fro.
Despair was on her cheek—and in her eye
A mother's anguish: "But they might have seen
How fierce a storm was gathering—might have stayed."
And while the hope was fresh within her heart
She hurried in, but only to return
And take her station at the door again.

　　* * * * * * * * *

The moments slowly lengthened into hours,
The air grew chilly—for upon the hearth
A few decaying embers smoked alone;
And pale with midnight vigils and with grief
The watcher knelt to find relief in prayer.
Then hark! a sound—a footstep—and she starts!
Her heart leaps to her throat, and with a bound
She gains the cottage door—it opens wide.

A cry of joy is trembling on her lips,
For there the husband and the father stood.
She stretched her eager arms to take the boy,
But in the movement caught the father's eye
Where horror sat, and told the dreadful tale
He dared not trust his quivering lips to speak.
"*My boy is dead,*" she cried; "my boy, my boy!"

And caught him wildly to her bursting heart.
Cold on her bosom fell the little head
Which had been pillowed there so oft in sleep,—
And as she raised the frosty lid which veiled
The violet eye beneath that lately laughed,
So deep a groan escaped her pallid lips
The guilty husband shuddered as he heard.
" Too late," he muttered in a husky tone,
And like an image of despair he stood,
Until she called him weeping to her side,
And murmured in a voice half choked with sobs:
" Nay, not too late, my husband, not too late :
God takes the child in mercy and in love,
To save the father. Shall it not be so ?
Say by the love we bore this precious child,
Our own no longer—shall it not be so ? "
The answer came, so low she scarcely heard,
But 'twas enough, and she looked up and smiled !

Sighs on Mortality.

WHAT IS YOUR LIFE?

Why do we mourn? why do we sigh?
We who may to-morrow lie
With folded hands and death-sealed eye?

A brave and gallant heart I knew:
Like some young sturdy oak he grew
Nursed by the sun, refreshed by dew.

His hopes were bright and high their aim:
Above reproach or fear of shame
None ever lightly spoke his name.

He left our cottage blithe and gay,
And as he left we heard him say,
"I will return at close of day."

We watched him as he passed along,
He was so manly, brave and strong,
Oh, was the pride we cherished wrong?

We thought of him as one designed
To bless and elevate mankind,—
And it was well that we were blind!

We did not see the gathering frown,—
But long before the sun went down,
A dreadful rumor filled the town.

They told us gently he was dead,—
I would not credit what they said:
But when I knew it reason fled.

I woke to real life once more;
My dream of happiness was o'er—
I stood upon a desert shore.

All day I heard the billows moan,
All night I answered groan with groan,
For I was desolate and lone.

There came no message o'er the sea,
No message from the lost to me,
And I repined at God's decree.

The bolt was spared—and o'er my head
The bow of mercy shone instead,
And I at last was comforted.

Now when the billows rage and roar,
I think it shortly will be o'er,—
'Tis calm upon the other shore.

I look at Time as one who sees
A pale leaf floating on the breeze
Amid a grove of noble trees.

It fills awhile a little nook;
To-day it is—to-morrow, look!
The great white Throne! the open Book!

We stand upon a narrow space,
Eternity rolls on apace—
Where next shall be our resting-place?

LIFE.

As when the graceful bark, with spreading sails,
   Glides from the port into the open sea,
Wafted along by soft and prosperous gales,

Just as the rising sun bids darkness flee;
So, like that bark, in early youth are we,
When first we launch upon the sea of life—
Our hopes as bright, our youthful souls as free,
The scene around with love and beauty rife.
And all unknown to us its griefs, its cares and strife.

The bark glides on; but, see, the azure sky
With dark and angry clouds is soon o'ercast;
The thunders roar, the forkèd lightnings fly,
The billows beat, and howls the midnight blast!
The trembling vessel, with dismantled mast,
The maddened waves have in their fury tossed,
Until she lies a helpless wreck at last,
Her plans all thwarted, and her hopes all crossed,
Her guiding star obscured, and her direction lost.

'Tis thus with life; at times deemed most secure,
When all seems calm, and beautiful, and fair,
Dark rocks concealed, the easier to allure,
The fragile bark in youth's bright morn ensnare;
And storms arise, and fierce the lightnings glare,
And wild and high the raging billows roll,
While sinks the heart a wreck in deep despair,
Till, brightly o'er the dark and dreary pole,
The Morning Star appears to the benighted soul!

It guides the bark across life's troubled sea,—
It points the way unto the destined shore,
Till, anchored in a blest eternity,
It buffets with the howling storm no more.
Be ours that star to guide us safely o'er!
To us, oh, may may its precious light be given!
And though the tempests beat and billows roar,
And though we now by adverse winds are driven,
We'll safely anchor soon in the blest port of Heaven!

THE SILENT ARMY.

Life is the road to death. No one can lose the way —'tis sure and plain. Whatever paths we take all end the same. Some walk in sunshine, and some beneath a cloud; some gather flowers and some the thorn; but at the gate all stand alike: nor poverty, nor wealth can enter there.

> To those who smile, and those who weep,
>   To those who sing, and those who sigh,
> There comes the same long final sleep,—
>   There comes the time when each must die.
>
> We watch the faces as they pass —
>   We say of some, "How very fair":
> Nor think how soon the churchyard grass
>   Will thrive upon the beauty there.
>
> The objects of our love we take
>   Close to our hearts and call them ours!
> They are the gods we ne'er forsake,
>   But crown them every morn with flowers.
>
> We dip them o'er and o'er again
>   In love's immortal fount; but when
> We find that all has been in vain,
>   God shield us in our anguish then.
>
> The Death-drum beats, the roll is called,
>   New names are on the list to-day:
> Some answer calm and unappalled
>   As if 'twere pleasure to obey.
>
> For life to them was full of pain,
>   Death opened wide the only door,

While others weep and plead in vain
  For just one little moment more.

Through all the springs that come and go,
  At noon, at night, at early dawn,
Through summer's heat and winter's snow,
  That silent army marches on!

On, on forever to the tomb!
  They pitch no tents along the way;
On, on, it is the common doom,
  There's no return and no delay.

They take no purse nor scrip with them
  However rich they were before;
The brow of beauty wears no gem,
  And slaves are men—and kings no more.

From every land, and sea, and clime,
  Through all the ages that are gone,
Through all the years of future time,
  That host has marched—will still march on.

And shall we of to-morrow boast?
  This very night may seal our doom
And find us with that shadowy host,
  Whose line of march is for the tomb!

Death and the tomb! our hearts rebel,
  And wonder why such things should be;
Great God, who doeth all things well,
  We leave these mysteries with Thee!

Thou knowest why, and we shall know
  When raised in triumph from the grave,
Redeemed from death, and sin, and woe,
  Through Him who hath the power to save.

THE DYING WARRIOR.

A warrior lay, with a heaving breast,
　On the field of the dying and dead;
His cheek was pale and his lips compressed,
And the fading light from the distant west
　Shone o'er his gory bed.

The night came on, and the moon arose
　With her soft and tremulous glow;
She shed her light o'er friends and o'er foes,
All sleeping together in dull repose
　On the battle-field below.

The warrior gazed with a mournful sigh
　On the blue and the star-spangled dome;
While tears shone bright in his sunken eye,
And vivid thoughts like the lightning fly
　To his childhood's distant home.

He thought of the mother who used to bend
　O'er his couch, when in sorrow and pain—
Who to his complaints an ear would lend;
But alas! he knew that that dearest friend
　Would never bend o'er him again.

He thought of the scenes where once he strayed
　With his brothers in days of yore;
He thought of the stream, the peaceful glade,
The cottage that stood in the dark green shade,
　With the vines around the door.

He thought, with a pang of dark despair,
　'Twas the hour they all used to meet
With grateful heart for the evening prayer;
He thought of the group that were gathered there;
　He thought—of a vacant seat.

He knew that a fervent prayer would rise
  For the loved and the long-absent one;
He knew that the tears would flow from their eyes,
And his father's voice would be choked with sighs,
  As he prayed for his erring son.

He knew for him they would all implore
  A renewed and a sanctified heart;
That when the toils of this life were o'er
They all might embrace each other once more,
  Never, no never to part!

One trembling hand to his brow he pressed,
  And the tears of contrition he shed;
He implored for pardon, a home with the blest;
Then he wrapped his cloak round his gory breast,
  And the warrior's spirit fled!

ON SEEING A SKULL.

This morning while examining a skull strange emotions took possession of me—such as I never before experienced. That senseless skull had once been the seat of deep thought and powerful passions; beaming eyes once glistened brightly where now there was only a hollow space; that head was once proudly erected, and the form that supported it once mingled in the busy scenes of life. But now what a change! His very name is forgotten—himself but a handful of dust. O mortals! behold, and learn a lesson. His body has long since mouldered away and mingled with the parent earth,—this skull alone remains; and yet the time will surely come, and cannot be far distant, when "the bones shall come together—bone to his bone"; when the sinews and the flesh shall come upon them, the skin cover them, and the breath entering the body the dead shall live! Will this skull come forward at "the resurrection of the just," or ———? Oh, what an awful thought! My very blood runs cold, and a shudder steals over me. O thou great Mediator of mankind, intercede for me before thy Father's throne, that ere it is everlastingly too late my unworthy name may be written in the Lamb's book of life. (*July* 5, 1852.)

THOUGHTS ON DEATH.

A bride but yesterday—all hope and love,—
Flowers at her feet and cloudless skies above,
Bright buds of promise twining round her brow,
Approach—approach and gaze upon her now!
Come not in festal robes as once ye came,
The bride is here but she is not the same
As when ye saw her to the altar led,
And called down blessings on her fair young head.
The cheek is pale that with the rose could vie,
There is no lustre in that rayless eye,
Upon those pallid lips there is no breath,
And she alas is now the bride of Death!
Henceforth what soul will ever dare to trust
In things that crumble at a breath to dust?
And who would dream of earthly joy and bliss
Taught by a lesson terrible as this?

Short-sighted mortal hastening to the tomb,
Gaze on the scene, and realize thy doom!
All tongues and nations mingle with the clay;
Art thou less subject unto death than they?
The conquerors of the world have left their throne
Before a mandate mightier than their own,—
Rank, pride and power have sunk into the grave,
And Cæsar moulders with the meanest slave.
Canst thou escape his all-destroying breath
And bid defiance to the victor Death?
What strange enchantment has allured thine eyes?
Shake off the spell! immortal soul, arise!
Oh, burst thy fetters ere it be too late,
Regain thy freedom and thy lost estate,—
A thousand angels hover round thy track,
They plead with thee, they long to lead thee back.

The sacrifice too great? bethink thee, soul!
A few more suns above thy head may roll,
A few at most and thou wilt trembling stand
Just on the borders of the spirit land.
Who ever stood there calm and undismayed,
And smiled to see all earthly prospects fade?
Not he who lived for things of time alone,
Who won a name, a fortune or a throne;
Who added field to field, and store to store,
And cried at last, "Oh, for one moment more!"
But he whose eye could pierce the dreary tomb,
He who could say amid the gathering gloom,—
"There is my home and there my Saviour stands
With smiling brow and with extended hands!"
Would'st thou depart with that exulting cry,
In glorious hope of immortality?
Thy heart all joy, and praise thy latest breath?
The holy life insures the happy death!
Oh, thou wilt wonder in that trying hour

When home, and love, and friendship lose their power
To cheer and comfort, thou could'st ever prize
What then will sink to nothing in thine eyes—
Time for repentance then ? beware ! beware !
How many souls are yearly shipwrecked there !
Like him of old they cry—" Go now thy way "—
And keep repentance for their dying day ;
But God is jealous of his honor still,
He asks a ready mind, a hearty will,
And those who through a life-time break his laws,
Despite his mercy and his glorious cause,
Who seek their own enjoyment and their ease,
And only yield when death demandeth these,—
May find too late they were deceived at last,
And mourn the summer and the harvest past !

There's not in heaven itself a lovelier sight,
Nor one which angels view with more delight,
Than youthful soldiers of Immanuel's cross,
In life's glad morning counting all as loss,
Since they have proved a dying Saviour's love,
And placed their treasures and their hearts above.
Let pleasure woo them with her syren voice,
They heed her not—they've made a nobler choice ;
Let others walk the shining path of fame,
They dare to suffer poverty and shame,
And turning from the world's enchanted bowers,
To consecrate their youth and all their powers
To Him they serve, and even here they find
More real pleasure than they e'er resigned.

The best they have in early life they bring
A free-will offering to their God and King ;
And in that hour when heart and flesh shall fail,
Their song of triumph ringing through the vale,
Will mingle with the anthems of the blest,

Who wait to hail them to their heavenly rest.
Would'st thou depart with that exulting cry
In glorious hope of immortality?
I read an answer in that beaming face,
Behold thy Saviour—fly to his embrace!

THE BATTLE-FIELD.

Strewn on the battle-plain,
After the fight was done,
And the bloody victory won,
Were a thousand heaps of slain.
Rider and horse there lay,
But the war-steed neighed no more,
And the gallant form he bore
Upon that eventful day,
Shattered, and marred, and ghastly pale,
Had fallen beneath the deadly hail.

Prince and peasant were there!
Rich and poor, master and slave,
Wise and simple, timid and brave;
Old men with snow-white hair,
Young men of noble birth,
Boys just from their native shore,
And the homes they shall see no more,
Stretched on the cold, damp earth;
And mother and sister may watch in vain,
They never shall press those lips again.

Clasped in a fond embrace
Was a young and gentle pair,
And the love that was pictured there
Made holy that dreadful place.
Near by a chieftain bled,

While his faithful dog still kept
A mournful watch where he slept,
And mourned above the dead,
Then gazed on the pallid lips and brow :
It is death—does he comprehend it now ?

Just as they fell they lay—
Struck down in the dreadful strife ;
And the latest look they wore in life
Death had not taken away :
Some with a pleasant smile,
Foeman with foemen at peace,
Croat, and Frank, and Tyrolese,
All in one ghastly pile,—
From the Seine, the Po, and the Land of Song,
Oh, where were the souls of that countless throng ?

Gone to the bar of God !
Gone from the battle's din,
Gone with their weight of sin,
To the solemn bar of God !
Woe to ambition and pride !
Woe to the tyrant king
Who dares from his subjects wring
What God has never denied !
Aye, woe to him, for the record stands,
And the blood of the slain is on his hands.

DEAD AND FORGOT.

Dead and forgot !
How sad the lot
When wintry tempests blow
To lie all cold
'Neath the churchyard mould,

And in a year or so
To have our very name unsaid,
Unless it chance to fall
From careless lips that say, " She's dead,"—
She's dead, and that is all!

But sadder still
That one should fill
The place we thought our own :
That a form more light,
And an eye more bright
Should guard our dear hearth-stone ;
That where we strayed another's feet
At morn and eve should roam,
And another's voice—perchance more sweet—
Make music in our home !

That where we locked
Our hands and talked
Amid our chosen flowers,
The lips we pressed
Should be caressed
By other lips than ours,—
That other eyes should watch for him,
And other arms embrace,
Until our image growing dim
Yield to another's face.

And this is love !
O injured Dove !
Thy wings have many a stain :
But pure and white
In the Land of Light
They shall be spread again ;
The deep, true love our spirits crave
Earth never has supplied ;

Nor till we leave the dreary grave
Shall we be satisfied.

DEAR EMILY.

Dear Emily, sweet Emily!
  So early gone to rest,
I love to think of thee as one
  Among the good and blest,—
No shadow on thy radiant eye,
  No sorrow in thy breast.

Dear Emily, sweet Emily!
  I cannot call thee dead:
'Tis true I do not see thy face
  Nor hear thy gentle tread;
Yet in my heart of hearts, sweet friend,
  Thou never canst be dead.

When by the solemn stream of death
  We parted long ago,
How little of the world we knew!
  But I have lived to know
How friendship fades, how love decays,
  How all things change below.

Time changes some, and absence some,
  And envy—oh, the shame!
Of those who played together once
  Some rise to wealth and fame,
While in the vale of poverty
  The rest remain the same.

But nothing now can come between
  Thy heart and mine, sweet friend!

With every image of the past
  Thy memory will blend,
And what thou wast in early life
  Thou wilt be to the end.

I love to think—oh, call it not
  A fancy wild and vain—
That thou hast seen and pitied me
  Through all these years of pain;
But I shall know how that has been
  When we two meet again.

My bleeding feet have left their mark
  Wherever they have passed;
But now the sun is getting low,
  The shadows lengthen fast,
And Emily, dear Emily,
  All will be well at last!

ON THE DEATH OF A FRIEND.

She sleeps the quiet sleep of death and I survive. But for what purpose? why was not I called first to explore the untried regions of eternity? 'Tis known only to Him whose mighty arm often spares the humble flower while the waving trees that stand around it are torn from their roots by the roaring tempest. She has gone before me, and yet how long may it be ere I shall follow her? O solemn thought!—well might it sink deeply into my heart, and taking root there spring forth yielding fruits of repentance. Soon may Death, the great enemy of mankind, add one more ghastly victim to the lifeless piles that lie heaped together in every clime and on every shore; and when my death-knell shall sound will it be the signal of a spirit wailing in the regions of the lost, or rejoicing in the bright realms of everlasting bliss? It is for me, and me alone to decide. Perhaps it is for this that my life has been spared—that I might make a firm and decided choice; and shall I still draw back? shall I still hesitate and remain inactive? No, no; for "now is the accepted time, and now is the day of salvation."

THE HEAVENLY HELPER.

What strange lessons I am every day learning! Thank God for them. They are very unpleasant to human nature, but they are leading me to place less confidence in earthly love and more in heavenly. I have leaned too much upon an arm of flesh, and it is right I should suffer for it. Sweet Saviour, fold me in thine arms; comfort me with thy love; and as soon as thou seest best let me go and live with thee forever.

All earthly hopes have passed away,
Stay with me, O my Saviour, stay:
Thy blessed smile is all the light
That breaks upon my dismal night.

I cling to thee—thou must not go;
Oh, let me tell thee every woe

And whisper in thy ready ear
What other friends would frown to hear.

Distressed in body and in mind,
Diseased and wretched, poor and blind,
I only care to see thy face,—
I only sigh for thy embrace.

I droop, I faint beneath the rod,
It is so heavy, O my God!
Spare me, I cry, in mercy spare,—
But thou refusest still the prayer!

Sometimes I murmur and repine,
Prefer my stubborn will to thine,
And doubt if love or anger deal
The dreadful anguish that I feel.

Then suddenly before me stands,—
With bleeding side, and feet, and hands,—
The Lamb that groaned and died for me,
That I might live eternally.

Such love o'erwhelms me, and with shame
I call upon thy holy name;
Forgive me, O thou blessed One,
And let thy will, not mine, be done.

O my Redeemer, Friend and Guide,
Take health, take what thou wilt beside,
But let me see the lovely face
That makes a heaven of every place.

Nay, turn not from my earnest prayer!
Thy smile can save me from despair;
The shadows deepen round my way,
Stay with me, O my Saviour, stay.

Who save thee, O God, knoweth the human heart? Pity me, for thy rod is heavy. My earthly hopes are all torn and crushed,—oh, may they turn heaven-ward and there find support and nourishment. This is Father's discipline, shall I murmur? Nay, but rather rejoice that he does not leave me to myself but deals with me as a child—chastening, rebuking, scourging and refining: preparing me by all these afflictions for the "rest that remaineth for the people of God." And sweet the rest will be after such a weary journey! How I shall fold my hands upon the bosom that shall never again be troubled, and say in all sincerity: I thank thee, O God, for the sweet that was mingled in my earthly cup, but more do I thank thee for the bitter.

THE PROMISE.

" In early life I'm called to part
    With all I hold so dear;
Strong tendrils bind my yearning heart,
    But cannot keep me here.

" I am resigned; yet tears will fall,
    Sad thoughts steal over me;
And dost thou know that with them all
    Are mingling thoughts of thee?

" We have been friends in hopes and fears
    In joys and griefs the same—
Since first we learned in childhood's years
    To lisp each other's name.

"In quiet grove, in lonely dell,
  In meadows green and fair,
Beside the stream we loved so well,
  If one then both were there.

"Together we our plans have laid
  With hopeful brow and heart,—
When roving 'neath the summer shade,
  But never thought to part.

"The spring will come, the trees will wave
  As when we saw them last,
But thou wilt linger by my grave,
  And muse upon the past.

"Beyond the portals of the tomb
  I look with joyful eye:
A glorious light dispels the gloom,
  'Tis not so hard to die.

"There is a home of rest divine—
  A home prepared for me;
But hours of darkness will be thine,
  For this I cling to thee.

"Hark! 'tis the angel choirs above;
  I've but one earthly care,—
Oh, promise me by all our love
  That thou wilt meet me there."

That earnest look—I see it still,
  That voice—I hear it yet;
And death this aching heart shall chill
  Before it can forget.

The flowers have faded one by one,
  The summer birds are flown,

And 'neath a cold autumnal sun
  I wander forth alone.

The yellow leaves are falling fast
  Along the river side,—
I watch them borne upon the blast,
  And on the swelling tide.

I think how all things earthly fade,
  Then wipe the tears that flow,
As memory brings the promise made
  So many years ago.

THE DEAD CHRIST.

The last expiring groan was hushed; the beaming eye was closed—it wept no longer over the sins of a perverse race. Those gentle and lovely features were robed with the pallid hue of death, and the heart that melted at the sorrows of mankind beat no longer. The grave, the cold grave, rejoicingly closed its dreary portals upon his sacred form; and he, the lowly and despised Nazarene, who found no resting-place for his weary head, slept quietly in a borrowed sepulchre.

THE COMPLAINT.

Ah! many springs have come and gone,
  And called me forth in vain;
Now winter folds the winding-sheet
  Round nature's breast again.

Young hands have gathered bright, wild flowers,
  Young feet have trod the grass,
But I have watched in solitude
  The mournful shadows pass.

Young hands have gathered brighter flowers
  From wisdom's pleasant tree—
But darker still the shadows fall,
  There are no flowers for me!

No flowers! where shadows deepest lie
  Amid the wint'ry gloom,
Thank God, I see with kindling eye
  The Rose of Sharon bloom!

It is enough—my earthly hopes
  Are fading one by one;
My God and my Redeemer lives,
  And may his will be done.

I know that in a better world
  I shall look back and say
I never could have reached my home
  By any other way.

And such a home! no frightful dreams,
  No wakings to despair—
No cries of—God remove the cup,
  Or give me strength to bear!

No pillows wet with burning tears,—
  No longings wild and vain
To wander in the pleasant fields,
  Or dear old woods again!

But love and peace, and endless joy,
  And rest to me how strange!

Lord give me patience to await
The happy, happy change!

THE MIXED CUP.

Joy and sorrow, are they not mingled in every cup? We call some happy, others unfortunate; and so they appear to us. But could we draw aside the curtain that conceals the mysteries of the human heart what problems would be solved, and how often we should be lead to exclaim, "God dealeth justly: pain and pleasure are more equally distributed than we imagined"! But this may not be. We judge according to appearances, and this is one great source of misery; for, in our grief, we imagine others are more favored than we, and for the blessings we do enjoy we are not thankful. Oh, the great mercy of God! What a wonder it is that he does not smite us to the earth when we dare murmur at his dealings!

I SHALL DEPART.

When the flowers of Summer die,
When the birds of Summer fly,
When the winds of Autumn sigh,
    I shall depart.

When the mourning Earth receives
Last of all the faded leaves,—
When the wailing forest grieves,
    I shall depart.

When are garnered grain and fruit,
When all insect life is mute,
I shall drop my broken lute;
    I shall depart.

When the fields are brown and bare,
Nothing left that's good or fair,
And the hoar-frost gathers there,
    I shall depart.

Not with you, O songsters, no!
To no Southern clime I go,—
By a way none living know
    I shall depart.

Many aching hearts may yearn,
Many lamps till midnight burn,
But I never shall return,
    When I depart.

Trembling, fearing, sorely tried,
Waiting for the ebbing tide,
Who, oh! who will be my guide
    When I depart?

Once the river cold and black
Rolled its waves affrighted back,—
I shall see a shining track
    When I depart.

There my God and Saviour passed,
He will be my guide at last,—
Clinging to his merits fast,
    I shall depart.

                —*Written in* 1858.

TIME FLIES.

Years are coming, years are going,
    Be they fraught with joy or pain,—
Like a river they are flowing
    To the everlasting main!

On the banks are thorns and roses,
    And we take of both a share
Till the ocean round us closes,
    And we drop our anchor—where?

If the future were uncertain,
    If across the mighty deep,
Brushing back the misty curtain
    Angel pinions did not sweep,—

If there were no bright to-morrow
    For our day of toil and strife,
Burdened with its weight of sorrow,
    What a curse were human life!

Locks are whitening, cheeks are paling,
    With each month and year that flies;
Youth and vigor both are failing,
    But the spirit never dies!

Short indeed is our probation,
    Dark and certain is the tomb,—
But the Lamp of revelation
    Dissipates the fearful gloom.

Oh, we take our life too sadly,
    Ever grieve and mourn too much,
Turn to ashes what would gladly
    Turn to gold beneath our touch.

'Tis because that in our blindness
    We imagine God is blind,—
'Tis because we doubt his kindness,
    That we cannot be resigned.

Nature cries amid the trials
    That beset our thorny path:
" God outpoureth all the vials
    Of his anger and his wrath!"

Such complaints are more surprising
    Since the declaration runs:
"If ye be without chastising,
    Then indeed ye are not sons."

All our future course He seeth
    Better than we see our past,
And whatever he decreeth
    We shall understand at last.

Let us then in our affliction
    Meekly trust our gracious Lord,—
Well assured his benediction
    Will ere long be our reward.

Let us beautify the present,—
    There is much we all can do
That will make the year more pleasant,
    For ourselves and others too.

A VOICE FROM A SICK-ROOM.

[At one time Miss JOHNSON seems to have entertained the idea of writing for publication a series of articles entitled " Voices from a Sick-room." Whether she ever wrote more than one or not I cannot say. The following is the only one we can find among her manuscripts, and it is so thrillingly interesting as to make us wish for more. It is dated Sept. 5, 1859.]

Draw the curtains—shut out the light of heaven; the inner world is so full of darkness that the sunshine of the outer world becomes painful by contrast. Hush, little bird! don't sing to-day. There—all is dark and still. Now, O wretched heart, exult in thy wretchedness; draw the dark, heavy curtains of despair around thee; shut out the light of hope and love; hush the voice of praise and thanksgiving. Think of all thou hast suffered; think of thy present misery; crowd the future with black-robed phantoms; people every nook and corner with horrible faces, and over all let the thunder crash and bellow, and the winds moan and shriek, as they moan and shriek only when the great are dying.

Ah, what sad havoc do sickness and pain make of the poor body; but sadder still when they trample on the bright inhabitant within, and make it a slave to tremble at their bidding! "Bring chains—bring chains," cries the fell destroyer; and ere she has time to rally her forces around her, or even think of resistance, the poor Soul has become a helpless captive, and Disease wears a smile of triumph upon her ghastly cheek, and again lifts up her voice to shout "victory." And a complete victory it is: Self-control, Pride, Ambition—all are humbled; Hope is shrouded in sackcloth, and if she ever speaks it is only to whisper: "There is one secret passage by which thou mayest yet escape, but it winds through the kingdom of Death and the Grave." Reason herself grows pale and trembles, lest she lose her throne; for the thousands of obedient servants, which have never before disputed her authority, are all up in arms against her. Every nerve begins to quiver and vibrate; the whole body is in commotion; and no wonder the trembling Soul sits down amid the ruins of her former self and makes the whole place doleful with her cries and lamentations.

Don't chide her: she is no criminal waiting the demands of justice, but a prisoner of war, and therefore should be dealt kindly with. Don't gaze at her through her prison bars, as though she were a wild beast caged, or some curious object kept only for a show; but go to her enveloped in the mantle of love, upon your lips the honey-dew of human kindness, and in your heart the melting tenderness of Christian affection. Don't tell her she is escaping many trials and temptations to which she would be exposed if she came in contact with the busy world around her. Go to the imprisoned eagle, and, as he looks up longingly into the deep blue sky and beats his wings in agony, comfort him with the assurance that his wants are provided for, and he himself safe from the arts of the fowler! Aye, tell this to the free-born eagle, but disgust not the ever-yearning, restless Soul with such mockeries. She may listen, but she laughs you to scorn in secret and prays Heaven to be delivered from such comforters. She knows her struggles and temptations are inward; and she knows too, for that very reason, they are more terrible. There greater battles have been fought than the blood-dyed fields of Europe ever witnessed. Magentas and Solferinas fatten with the blood of heroes, but she carries on a never ending warfare "with principalities and powers"—the numberless host of hell—and legions of native passions.

Deal gently with her. Would you win her confidence? There is but one passage to her affections. Speak that word—bolt and bar fly open: she takes you by the hand and welcomes you to her most sacred and secluded retreat. That word is *sympathy:* let her feel it in your tender embrace, see it in the glance of your eye, hear it in the modulation of your voice. It is for this she yearns and sighs, and refuses to be comforted where it is not.

Bring her flowers—sweet, beautiful flowers. They are meet companions for her solitude. Gather blossoms from the whitening apple-bough, violets from the meadow, dandelions from the wayside. She will fold them more tenderly to her bosom than the rarest plants, for their faces are old, familiar ones, and she imagines they wear a look of pity.

But there are more precious things than human sympathy; there are sweeter flowers than violets or roses. They bloom on the prayer-consecrated mountains of Judea, amid the ancient olives of Gethsemane, along the Dolorous Way trodden by the Man of Sorrows, beneath the shadows of the Cross, and around the borrowed Sepulchre. Oh, gather them with no sparing hand: there are enough for you and her—enough for every sorrowing heart in the universe. Take them to the poor sufferer. Their fragrance will make the lonely chamber like a garden of spices; the tearful eyes will turn heavenward, and the pale lips—tremulous with contrition will whisper, "Father, forgive me, for I knew not what I did when I murmured at thy dealings." Then a solemn hush will follow—a holy twilight of the soul,—as if the sorrows of earth were blending with the joys of heaven, the pains of mortality with the blessedness of the angelic bards. Oh, these are the flowers for a sickroom! How dreary and desolate does it seem without them! The strong and healthy may live on, careless and irreligious, but what would become of the poor, grief-stricken, despairing Soul if she could not repose quietly in the bosom her Beloved, and say with child-like simplicity, morning and evening, "*Our Father who art in heaven!*"

Songs of Hope.

"HE GIVETH SONGS IN THE NIGHT."

Gloriously the sun sinks behind the western hills. Half the sky seems on fire, and the other half wreathed with light fantastic clouds. All nature is beautiful—can I be sad? Nay; away with sadness, away with sorrow; I will forget everything—my strangeness, my blasted hopes, and seek for happiness where happiness only is to be found, in the sacred Oracles of God.—*July* 14, 1852.

> God sometimes speaks in earthquake and in storm,
> But oftener in the "still small voice" of love:
> He urges men as loving fathers plead.
> God *is* our Father, yet we shun his face
> And hide ourselves when at the cool of day
> He walketh in the garden!

How sweet the thought that God, our heavenly Father, is omniscient. Our griefs are not hidden from him. He knows our hearts, and with all this knowledge he is good—so tender, so pitiful! Oh, to love him as he deserves! Oh, for a thousand tongues to sing his praises! Tell the sick, tell the sorrowing, tell the broken-hearted of this God; tell the wretched, the guilty, the wayward prodigal of this gracious Father.

THE LAST GOOD NIGHT.

[In the day of health and prosperity everybody feels like singing, but "in the night" of adversity grace must produce the song of holy confidence and hope. Such a song is the following, which has probably been printed oftener than any other of Miss Johnson's poems. It has appeared in several papers; finds a place in Dewart's "Selections from Canadian Poets"; was set to music by George F. Root, and appears in his "School for the Cabinet Organ." With many it has been a favorite.]

Mother, good night! my work is done,—
I go to rest with the setting sun:
But not to wake with the morning light,
So, dearest mother, a long good night!

Father, good night! the shadows glide
Silently down to the river's side,—
The river itself with stars is bright,
So, dearest father, a long good night!

Sisters, good night! the roses close
Their dewy eyes for the night's repose—
And a strange, damp mist obscures my sight,
So, dearest sisters, a long good night!

Brothers, good night! the sunset flush
Has died away, and a midnight hush
Has settled o'er plain and mountain hight,
So, dearest brothers, a long good night!

Good night! good night! nay, do not weep:
I'm weary of earth, I long to sleep—
I shall wake again with the dawning light
Of eternal day—good night, good night!

RETROSPECTIVE AND PROSPECTIVE.

I remember the time when we went forth arm in arm over the newly mown fields, scaring the grasshoppers from our pathway, with our baskets on our arms, to gather the blueberries that hung in clusters on their slender stalks. But thou art gone now to the fairer fields of paradise, to pluck sweeter fruit than ever ripened here. Thou art gone! The blueberry bushes have fallen long ago before the scythe; the field has changed its appearance; and as for me, the breezes woo me forth in vain—I cannot go. Sickness and sorrow have come between me and the love of earth; they have cast a dark shadow over what I once thought fair. But as there can be no shadow without a light beyond it I have caught bright glimpses of a better home—a land of life and glory.

HOPE.

[We have no clue to the time when this was written. It is imperfect: the second verse is not complete in the copy. But is it not true to life so far as earthly hope is concerned? Of "the hope of the gospel" our songstress would speak differently.]

What a syren is Hope—what a charming deceiver!
She whispers so blandly you can but believe her;
The garments of Truth and of Reason she stealeth
And every deformity thus she concealeth.

When down in the valley I'm talking with Sorrow
She comes with a song—all its burden *to-morrow;*
She mocks my companion . . . . .

Then she beckons me up to the top of a mountain;
She brings me a draught from a clear, sparkling fountain,
And talks of the beautiful prospect before us
Till ere I'm aware the dark night settles o'er us.

Sometimes in my anger I try to elude her;
I call her a jade and an idle intruder;
But she kisses, caresses, and coaxes, and flatters
Till I build me a castle the next zephyr shatters.

When I firmly resolve I will listen no longer,
Than my will or my reason somehow she is stronger:
I chide her, deride her, despise her and doubt her,
And yet it is true I can't live without her!

EARTH NOT THE CHRISTIAN'S HOME.

Earth, with all thy grief and sorrow,
And thy changes of to-morrow;
With thy woe and with thy parting,
With thy tears of anguish starting,
With thy countless heart-strings breaking,
With thy loved and lost forsaking,
With thy famished millions sighing,
With thy scenes of dead and dying,
With thy graveyards without number,
Where the old and youthful slumber;
Earth, oh, earth! thus dark and dreary,
Cold, and sad, and worn, and weary,
　　Thou art not my home!

Earth, oh, earth! with all thy slaughter
And thy streams of blood like water
O'er the field of battle gushing,

Where the mighty armies rushing,
Reckless of all human feeling,
With the war trump loudly pealing,
And the gallant banners flying,
Trample on the dead and dying;
Where the foe, the friend, the brother,
Bathed in blood sleep by each other;
Earth, oh, earth! thus dark and gory,
Blood and tears make up thy story,
   Thou art not my home!

Earth, with all thy scenes of anguish,
Where the poor and starving languish,
To the proud oppressor bending,
And their cries for mercy blending;
Where the slave with bosom swelling,
Which despair has made its dwelling,
And the scalding tear-drops falling—
Sight to human hearts appalling—
Strives, but strives in vain to sever
Fetters that must bind him ever;
Earth, oh, earth! with each possession
Sold to tyrants and oppression,
   Thou art not my home!

Earth, oh, earth! thy brightest treasures,
Like thy hopes and like thy pleasures,
Wintry winds are daily blighting;
Pain, and woe, and death uniting,
Youth and love and beauty crushing,
And the sweetest voices hushing;
Rich and poor, and old and blooming,
To one common mansion dooming;
While the cries of every nation
Mingle with those of creation;
Earth, oh, earth! thus dark and dreary,

Cold, and sad, and worn and weary,
   Thou art not my home!

Earth, oh, earth! though dark and gory,
In thy pristine state of glory
Angels came upon thee gazing,
Songs of love and rapture raising;
For thou then wast bright and beaming,
With the sunlight on thee streaming,
With thy crystal waters laving
Shores with fadeless forests waving;
With thy plains and with thy mountains,
With thy ever-gushing fountains;
Earth, oh, earth! once fair and holy,
Fallen, fallen, and so lowly;
   Thou art not my home!

Earth, oh, earth! bowed down by sorrow,
Cheer thee, for there comes a morrow;
Night and clouds, and gloom dispersing,
And thyself, O earth, immersing
In a flood of light undying;
When the curse upon thee lying,
With its thousand woes attending,
Death, and pain, and bosoms rending,
Partings that the heart-strings sever,
Will be banished and forever,—
Earth, oh, earth! renewed in glory,
Love and joy make up the story;
   Oh, be thou my home!

Earth, although thou seem'st forsaken,
Yet a note of praise awaken;
For the angels, lowly bending
Round the throne of light unending,
Gaze upon thee, sad and groaning,

Listen to thy bitter moaning;
Thou hast scenes to them amazing,
While on Calvary's mountain gazing;
And they smile on every nation
Purchased with so great salvation,—
Earth, oh, earth,! renewed in glory,
Angels shall rehearse thy story;
   Oh, be thou my home!

Earth, the morn will *soon* break o'er thee,
And thy Saviour will restore thee;
Far more bright and far more blooming,
And more glorious robes assuming
Than when first, o'er Eden ringing,
Angel-voices were heard singing;
For thy King himself descending,
Heaven and earth together blending,
With his saints a countless number,
Those who live and those who slumber,
Over thee will reign victorious,—
Earth, oh, earth, thus bright and glorious,
   Be thou then my home!

"WE SORROW NOT AS OTHERS WITHOUT HOPE."

While looking over an old manuscript, written by one who is long since passed from time into eternity, I met with the following lines: "It is six years to-day since my Elsa died, and five months since my Amanda left me forever. They sleep in the grave, and there they will remain through endless years." He then went on, in strains mournful and tender, and with all a father's sorrow deplored his loss. I could not wonder that he wept the tears of anguish and despair if, as he said, they are to remain in the dark tomb through endless years. The glorious Resurrection morning was unknown to him. He saw only the tomb, and considered not that there is One who holds the keys of the grave, and who will soon burst the icy bars of death and bring forth the righteous to immortality. Truly that morning has charms for the Christian. God grant that if I am called to slumber for a while I may "have part in the first resurrection."—*June 22, 1852.*

THE MESSENGER BIRD.

Oh, fly away to the better land,
  Thou bird of the snowy wing!
Oh, fly away to the blood-washed band,
  And hear the songs they sing!

But bear a message from us, O dove,
  To that bright and happy throng;
For we have friends whom we dearly love,
  Who swell the Conqueror's song.

Oh tell them our hearts are sad and lone,
  Our homes not bright as of yore;
For we miss the soft, the soothing tone
  Of the friends we loved before.

Oh tell them we sigh for the better land,
  For earth has grown sad and chill;
And we long rejoicing with them to stand
  On the heights of Zion's hill.

Oh tell them we long to share their rest,
  Afar from all earthly strife;
We long to lean on our Saviour's breast,
  And roam by the tree of life.

Oh tell them our fondest hopes are there,
  For our earthly hopes are o'er;
And we sigh for the land all bright and fair—
  We sigh for the deathless shore.

Then fly away to the better land,
  Thou bird of the snowy wing!
Oh fly away to the blood-washed band,
  And hear the songs they sing.

And then return with the speed of love,
  When the night grows dark and chill,
And tell us, oh, tell us, thou white-winged dove!
  Do they love, do they love us still?

We know there is One, in that blissful home,
  Who loves and remembers us yet;
Though weary and sorrowful now we roam,
  We know that he will not forget.

We'll trust him then, the great and the strong;
  By his own almighty hand
He'll bring us soon with the blood-washed throng
  To the bright, the better land.

OUR SHIP IS HOMEWARD BOUND.

What though the angry waves are high,
  And darkness reigns around?
Let hope be bright in every eye,
  Our ship is homeward bound!

What though nor moon nor stars appear
    Amid the gloom profound,
Why should we yield a place to fear?
    Our ship is homeward bound!

What though the lightnings glare above,
    And deaf'ning thunders roar,
When with the eye of faith and love
    We view the distant shore?

We know that friends are waiting there
    We loved in life before;
And angel forms all bright and fair
    Line the eternal shore.

We've often longed with them to bow
    At our Redeemer's feet,—
He loved us first, we love Him now,
    Then let the billows beat!

And let them bear our hopes away,
    Although they once were sweet,
We catch a glimpse of coming day—
    Oh, let the billows beat!

The coward peers with trembling form
    Into the gloom profound,
But we can smile to view the storm,
    Our ship is homeward bound!

And though for us on life's dark wave
    No anchorage be found,—
Oh, let our hearts be true and brave,
    Our ship is homeward bound!

MIDNIGHT.

Shades of night have gathered round,
'Tis the hour of gloom profound ;
'Tis the hour when many sleep,
'Tis the hour when many weep,
Over pleasures buried deep.

Faces smiling through the day,
Lips that told a spirit gay,
Eyes that beamed *as with* delight,
Now concealed from human sight,
Put aside the mask to-night.

Tossing on the couch of pain,
Seeking rest but all in vain,
With the dark and dreary tomb
Oft appearing through the gloom,
Weary sufferers wait their doom !

Bright and golden dreams have some :
On their airy wings they come,
Giving fancy leave to soar
To the happy scenes of yore,—
Or to some untraveled shore.

By the hearth he holds so dear,
Softly ringing in his ear
Gentle voices, faces bright
Bursting on his gladdened sight,—
Sits the wanderer to-night.

Clasping hands in holy trust
Long since mouldered into dust,—
Gazing into death-sealed eyes,
With a look of sweet surprise,
Every tear the mourner dries.

From some rugged mountain high
Making journeys through the sky,
Or in amaranthine bowers
Talking with the birds and flowers,
Poets spend the midnight hours.

Phantoms that by day elude,
Flying ever when pursued,—
Like the desert mirage bright,
Filled with joy and with delight
Dreamers fondly clasp to-night.

Oh, that morning's early beam
Should dissolve the blissful dream!
Oh, that love and hope should fly
Like the mist in yonder sky,
When the burning sun is high!

There's a morning yet to break,
When the sleepers shall awake
From the couch and from the grave,
From the mountain and the cave,
From beneath the ocean wave.

Then the *dream* of life is o'er,
Then they wake to sleep no more;
Then all earthly hopes shall fly
Like the mist in yonder sky,—
And that morning draweth nigh!

EASTER SUNDAY.

The old, the young, and the middle-aged all meet to-day in the house of prayer. From a thousand churches in our own and other lands the voice of praise and thanksgiving goes up to heaven—"*The Lord is risen!*" Oh glorious tidings! "The Lord is risen indeed," and hath appeared to Peter! aye, and to Mary also,—the poor sinner whose touch would have been profanation to the Pharisees of our own times. And still more wonderful, He hath appeared to Thomas—to Thomas the infidel, who laughed at the story of the resurrection!

THE RISEN REDEEMER.

Rejoice now, O sorrowing bride, for he sleeps no longer. Let thy glad songs of praise and adoration reach the skies, for thy Lord is not among the dead—he is risen. "Rejoice greatly, O daughter of Zion! shout, O daughter of Jerusalem!" for thy Saviour has burst the iron bands of death and come forth a mighty conqueror. For thy sins he laid himself down in the icy tomb; he rises again for thy justification. For thy iniquities he suffered, died and was buried: he comes forth again that thou mayest be a sharer of his glory. He has hallowed the dreary tomb by his own dear presence, and now he has ascended to his Father and your Father, to his God and your God. He has taken his seat at the right hand of the Majesty on high, and there, despairing soul, trembling under the burden of sin, he pleads for thee (Heb. 7 : 25). He points to the cross on Calvary, dripping with his own precious blood, and in a voice of tender compassion exclaims: "Father, I died for that

wretched sinner; spare, oh spare him for my sake!"
He has entered into the holy place by his own blood,
having obtained eternal redemption for thee, O daughter of Zion.

DOST THOU REMEMBER ME?

O Thou whose footsteps are unknown,
    Whose path is on the sea,—
Whose footstool earth, and heaven whose throne,
    Dost Thou remember me?

O Thou whom winds and waves obey,
    At whose supreme command
The shining worlds pursue their way,
    Or in their orbits stand,—

Thou at whose touch the hills disperse,
    And burning mountains flee,
Thou Ruler of the Universe,
    Dost Thou remember me?

This world though fallen still is thine,
    And dearer far to-day
Than all the countless orbs that shine
    But never went astray.

For here the blessed Son of God
    Was born, and wept, and died;
Our valleys and our hills he trod,
    And they are sanctified.

On Him my guilty soul relies,
    Through him I come to thee;
Thou dost accept my sacrifice,
    Thou dost remember me!

'T IS I—BE NOT AFRAID.

Dark hung the clouds o'er Galilee;
A lonely bark was on the sea,
   Where wild the billows played;
Deep terror filled each trembling frame,
When suddenly the accents came,
   "'T is I—be not afraid!"

A martyr stood with tranquil air;
He saw the stake, the fetters there,
   The fagots all arrayed;
But, though such darkness reigned around,
He caught the sweet, the cheering sound,
   "'T is I—be not afraid!"

A weary pilgrim roamed alone;
For him was breathed no friendly tone,
   No friendly hand brought aid;
But through the gloom so dark and drear,
A gentle whisper reached his ear,
   "'T is I—be not afraid!"

A mother knelt in anguish wild
Beside a loved, a dying child,
   And tears in torrents strayed;
A soothing voice breathed to her heart,
In tones that bade despair depart,
   "'T is I—be not afraid!"

Upon a bed of pain and death
A Christian faintly drew his breath,
   With spirit half dismayed;
He heard a soft, a tender voice—
It caused that spirit to rejoice—
   "'T is I—be not afraid!"

A penitent with streaming eye
Raised unto heaven his doleful cry,
  And fervently he prayed;
A brilliant light around him shone,
And with it came a heavenly tone,
  "'T is I—be not afraid!"

And when the trump from yonder skies
Shall bid the silent dead arise;
  When suns and stars shall fade;
When thunders roar, and mountains fall;
The saints shall hear above them all,
  "'T is I—be not afraid!"

THE ONLY PERFECT ONE.

I have just finished "D'Aubigné's History of the Reformation." How many noble characters are here brought to light! how many fervent Christians—how many lofty souls—how many holy hearts! The firm and undaunted Luther, the gentle Melancthon, the brave and courageous Zwingle, the mild Ecolampadius, the zealous and fiery Farel—and a host of others equally noble in the Master's cause. And yet they all had their faults; not one of them was perfect. Though we may sometimes feel to deplore their failings, yet surely it is a comfort to the poor Christian, beset with temptations and wandering daily from the straight and narrow path, to look back upon the lives of the best of earth's sons—the noblest and the holiest,—and behold that even they sometimes went astray. It buoys up his soul with new hope and courage. It bids it cast aside every thought of justification save by faith in Jesus Christ. It increases that faith, and directs the weary pilgrim to the feet of Him who alone is holy and perfect.—*June* 30, 1852.

THE DYING CHRISTIAN.

I have heard music from a far-off land,
    Where sighs and sad laments are never heard;
Where friends can meet and clasp each other's hand,
    But ne'er give utterance to that dreadful word
Which has wrung hearts, and like a funeral knell
Has tolled for our departed hopes—"*Farewell!*"

I have had visions of that blessed clime,
    Where fadeless flowers and fruits immortal grow—
Far, far beyond the troubled waves of Time,
    Where streams of living waters sparkling flow;
And while a pilgrim here I sadly roam,
I love to call that blissful land my home.

And often with the passing breeze I hear
    A sweet, a sad, perchance a warning tone:
"Heaven calls for thee," falls on my willing ear;
    Oh! can the glorious message be mine own?
Can it be mine, unworthy child of clay,
To win the realms of everlasting day?

Through Him who died, through Him who rose again,
    Through Him who lives, and lives forevermore,
I may at last that blissful rest obtain,
    And I may stand upon the lovely shore
Where youth and health on every cheek shall bloom,
Beyond the reach of death and of the tomb.

Then hail sweet voice! sweet message to my heart!
  Hail, land of love and home of endless peace!
Ye ties that bind me here, oh! quickly part,
  And shout, my soul, for joy to find release,
With angels meet and sing in sweet accord,
Forever blest, forever with the Lord!

THE REQUEST.

Come sit here close beside me and take my hand in
    thine,
And tell me of the happy home I think will soon be
    mine;
Oh, tell me of the river and of the garden fair,
And of the tree of life that waves its healing branches
    there!

And tell me of the love of God who gave his only Son
To die and suffer on the cross for deeds that I have
    done;
And tell to me the holy words the blessed Jesus spake
When from the courts of Heaven he came, an exile
    for my sake.

I love to hear how Mary sat at the Redeemer's feet,—
I wish I could have been there too, I would have
    shared her seat;
I envy much the little group that met at Martha's
    board
To listen to the gentle voice of him whom they
    adored.

I envy those rude fishermen who rowed him o'er the
    sea,
Who walked with him and talked with him as I now
    talk to thee;

I envy those who brought their sick, just at the close
   of day,
That they might be restored to health when Jesus
   passed that way.

Had I been living then I know I would have joined
   the crowd,—
"Have mercy, oh have mercy, Lord!" I would have
   cried aloud.
Thou sayest that I still may go and tell him all my
   grief,
And go I will; "Lord, I believe, help thou my unbe-
   lief."

I know my heart is very hard, I feel the load within;
But in the blood of Jesus Christ I wash away my sin;
I lay my burden at his feet while to his cross I cling;
I do so long to hear him speak death seems a blessed
   thing.

Now kneel here close beside me and lift thy voice in
   prayer
That I may say his will be done whatever I may bear,
Oh, I should love to *work* for him, if that could be his
   will,
But pray that I may be resigned—may suffer and be
   still.

COMPLETE IN HIM.

Does not the blood of Jesus alone cleanse from *all* sin?—who but sinners are invited to the great Fountain? Are my robes filthy?—where can they be made white but in the blood of the Lamb.? Is my heart obdurate and unbelieving?—who can soften and subdue it save the Almighty One who listens to its throbbings and knows all its trouble? Am I tempted, sorely tempted?—who can pity like Him who in the wilderness met face to face the great enemy, the great tempter of mankind? Ah, my poor heart aches when I think of all that is in the past and of all the future may have in store for me. But is there no balm in Gilead? is there no physician there? Will He not take me by the hand and whisper, "Be of good cheer; thy sins are forgiven thee"? Will He not heal thy wounds by pouring into them the oil of consolation? He has promised to do this—yea, much more than this; and will he for the first time in the history of mankind fail to perform what he has spoken? Nay, *nay*, and I will doubt no longer. . . . O Jesus, my Mediator, my Redeemer, have compassion upon me, and declare thyself to the Father as THE LORD MY RIGHTEOUSNESS.—*Sept.* 1860.

TRUST IN GOD.

Trust in God! He will direct thee,
He will love and will protect thee;
  Lean upon his mighty arm,
  Fear no danger, fear no harm.
Trust him for his grace and power;
Trust him in each trying hour.

Trust in God whate'er betide thee!
Trust him though he sometimes chide thee:

'Tis in love to lead thee back
When thou turnest from the track.
Trust him, cling to him forever,
And he will desert thee—never.

Trust in God, the Rock of ages!
Louder still the tempest rages,
   Earthquakes heave and thunders roar,
   Mountain surges lash the shore,
Nations tremble—hark! the warning,
"Comes the night, and comes the morning."

Watchmen on the walls of Zion
Catch a glimpse of Judah's Lion!
   Man of sorrows, Lamb once slain,
   Comes as King of kings to reign,
And from long oppressed Creation,
Break the anthems of salvation.

Trust in God! the morn awaits thee,
And while such a hope elates thee,
   Wilt thou fold thy hands in ease?
   No, the golden moments seize!
Lay thy gift upon the altar,
Thou hast duties—do not falter!

A PARADOX.

Alone, and yet not alone am I; sad, and yet not sad. No human form intrudes upon my solitude, and yet He who fills creation with himself is surely with me; sad I am, for there are many *earthly* thoughts that contribute to cast a shade upon my soul, and yet *heavenly* thoughts soon dispel such mournful ones.

Oh, that my whole affection might be placed upon things above, and not on things on the earth! Why should my heart be gloomy when such a glorious prospect opens before me?—a world of immortal beauty, enlivened by the presence of God himself, and a glorious city, even the New Jerusalem. "Fly, lingering moments, fly away, and bring that long expected day" when Christ shall appear in glory to take his weary children home.

"THOU SHALT KNOW HEREAFTER."

The wind has ceased—how still and tranquil all!
The ghastly moon still shines upon the wall;
While other eyes are closed why do I weep?
Begone, ye phantoms, welcome, balmy sleep!
And bear me to the shadowy land of dreams
Where yesternight I roamed by crystal streams,
And gathered flowers methought would never fade,
Or talked with angels 'neath the pleasant shade!

It was a dream; ah, yes, and life to me
Was once a dream—smooth as the placid sea
When all is calm, and on its bosom lies
The golden radiance of the summer skies.
There came a storm—the thunder's dreadful roar,
The angry waves that beat against the shore
Awakened me—oh, I had lived too long
In the bright realms of fancy and of song.

Perhaps 'twas well the storm swept o'er the sea,
Perhaps 'twas well the tumult startled me,
'Twas well I learned there's much to do and dare,

Much to be suffered, much to meekly bear,
But when I found the real though unsought,
And thought of life and trembled as I thought,—
When like the leaves in autumn day by day
The hopes I cherished hastened to decay,
And hopeless, helpless in my great despair
I turned to earth but found no solace there,
'Twas well for me that in the darkened skies
I saw the Star of Bethlehem arise!

I know not why, though nature craves to know,
That all my dreams of happiness below
Should be thus blighted, yet the time is near
When I, poor voyager, often shipwrecked here,
Shall reach the port, and safely moored at last
Review the scenes and sufferings of the past,—
Beholding where the shadows darkest lay
The dawning glory of immortal day,
And all along the path that seemed so drear
Leaving this one memorial—God was here!

"THINE EYES SHALL SEE THE KING IN HIS BEAUTY."

The thought is ever present, Shall these eyes indeed see the Maker of the universe? shall these feet indeed walk the Golden City? shall these hands wave the palm of victory and strike the chords of the glorious harp whose music shall be sweeter than that of David's? Can this be possible, and do I weep and mourn because of present affliction? Oh, the future, the future! what has it not in reserve for me? Glories of which mortal never dreamed: eternal life—eternal happiness—perpetual youth—knowledge unbounded, yet ever increasing! Fly, fly, fly, days of pain and sorrow! Hail, all hail! bright morn of deliverance. It *will* come; and I—oh, the thought overpowers me—I, poor and wretched and sinful, shall be blessed forever, *forever*, FOREVER.

ALL IS WELL.

Dark the future yawns before me,
    Bitter griefs my bosom swell;
But a light is breaking o'er me,
    And a voice—" All, all is well!"

Sad and lone has been my journey,
    Sad and lone my way must be:
Care and sorrow, pain and sickness,
    Long have been allotted me.

Sunshine that o'er youthful bosoms
    Flings a bright and magic spell,
Seldom breaks upon my pathway,
    Yet I know that all is well!

If the Hand that guides the planets
    Feeds the ravens when they cry,
Can it be that I'm unnoticed
    By a Father's loving eye?

He has thoughts of mercy toward me,
    His designs I cannot tell;
'Tis enough for me to trust Him,
    He knows best—and all is well!

Many doubts and many shadows
    Oft have flitted through my mind,

And I've questioned, sadly questioned,
    But no answer could I find.

Earth was silent to my pleading,
    Nature taught me to rebel;
But when I recall the promise
    "*I am with thee*"—all is well!

Many things I can't unravel;
    Many winding mazes see;
But I'll go with faith unshaken,
    For the Lord is leading me.

And when beams of endless glory
    The mysterious clouds dispel,
Grateful shall I tell my story,
    Grateful say that all was well!

WE SHALL MEET.

We have wandered oft together
    At the hour of setting sun;
Shall we wander thus together,
    When the toils of life are done?

Many hours we've spent together
    Scenes of joy and grief have known;
Shall we spend the hours together
    When the joy will be alone?

Sad indeed would be our parting
    If we hoped to meet no more,
But although the tears are starting,
    Look we to a brighter shore.

Dark indeed would be the morrow
  When apart we sadly roam,
If beyond this world of sorrow
  We could see no happier home.

But we've heard a joyful story
  Of a land that's bright and fair,
And we hope to share its glory,
  And to meet each other there.

Swiftly onward to the ocean
  Roll the troubled waves of time,
Bearing us with every motion
  Nearer to the blessed clime.

Soon the tears that now are starting
  With their causes will be o'er;
Soon the hands now clasped in parting
  Will be joined forevermore.

We have shared one home together,
  We have sat around one board;
And we'll find a home together
  In the Paradise restored!

WHAT THE DAUGHTER OF THE CLOUD SAID.

Down the spout a torrent gushed, to be pent up in an old, dark tub, and made the slave of the washerwoman. Would it not have been better for thee, O water, to have fallen in the beautiful forest? to lie in the bosom of the lily, or become a looking-glass for the many colored insects? "I would be useful," whispered the daughter of the cloud, "therefore I have stooped to an humble action—I left the abode of the lightning. My lot is a lowly one; my life full of sorrow and humiliation. I must pass through a fiery ordeal; I must be cast out and despised by those whom I have served. But then will be the time of my exaltation: the blessed Sun will take pity upon me, and make me a gem of beauty in the angels' highway!"

[Though no application has been made of this similitude, yet the truth designed to be taught is easily gathered: The Christian may be called to many a lowly act—to a ministration which will subject him to reproach and suffering here, but the day of exaltation is sure to come. "He that humbleth himself shall be exalted." The day hastens when from the heavens the Saviour will descend, "who will transform the body of our humiliation, that it may be conformed to the body of his glory."—Phil. 3 : 21 (*Am. Bible Union Trans.*). How glorious will the humble workers of earth appear when they are beautified by the Sun of righteousness in the resurrection morning! That will be an Easter day of surpassing loveliness.]

THIS IS NOT HOME.

This is not home! from o'er the stormy sea
Bright birds of passage wing their way to me;
They bear a message from the loved and lost
Who tried the angry waves and safely crossed,
And now in homelike mansions find repose
Where billows never roar nor tempest blows.

As strangers here in foreign lands we roam,
Oh, why should not the exile sigh for home?

A thousand snares beset our thorny way,
And night is round us—why not wish for day?
The storm is high, beneath its wintry wing
The blossom fades—oh, why not wish for Spring?

The waters roll o'er treasures buried deep,
And sacred dust the lonely churchyards keep—
Homes are dissolved and ties are rent in twain,
And things that charm can never charm again,
On every brow we mark the hand of time,
Oh, why not long for the celestial clime?

Wave after wave rolls inward to the land,
Then comes the wail and then the parting hand,
And those for whom we would have freely died
Are borne away upon the ebbing tide;
We weep and mourn, we bid the sea restore,
It mocks our grief—and takes one idol more.

'Tis well for us that ties which bind the heart
Too strongly here are rudely snapped apart;
'Tis well the pitcher at the fountain breaks,
The golden bowl is shattered for our sakes,
To show how frail and fleeting all we love,
To raise our souls to lasting things above.

We are but pilgrims—like the tribes who roam
In every land but call no land their home,—
And what their ancient Canaan is to them,
So is to us the New Jerusalem;
Then while our hopes, our hearts, our homes are there,
"*Thy Kingdom come*" must be our fervent prayer!

THE SOUL'S CONSOLATION.

Ah, well it is for thee that there is one ear that will listen, one eye that pities, one heart that will take thee in—"Thou God seest me!" Was ever consolation contained in so few words? Oh, repeat it when the heart is breaking—when between thee and every earthly object yawns a gulf dark and impassable. Thou God *seest* me! Thou God *lovest* me—lovest *me!* Thou knowest the agony of my spirit: thou knowest what I suffer, and thou must give me strength and grace to endure all, and to say in truth and sincerity, Thy will not mine be done.

"WE SEE THROUGH A GLASS, DARKLY."

We weep when from the darkened sky
    The thunderbolts are driven,
And wheresoe'er we turn our eye
    Our earthly hopes are riven;
But could we look beyond the storm
    That threatens all before us,
We might observe a heavenly form
    Guiding the tempest o'er us.

The eye that sees the sparrow's fall,
    That never sleeps nor slumbers,
Beholds our griefs however small,
    And every sigh he numbers.
The angels fly at his command,
    With love their bosoms swelling,
They lead us gently by the hand,—
    They hover round our dwelling.

And when the fading things of earth
    Our hearts too fondly cherish,
Forgetful of their mortal birth,

How suddenly they perish!
But 'tis in mercy and in love
　Our Father thus chastises,
To fix our thoughts on things above;
　He strikes, yet sympathizes.

We know not, and we may not know
　Till dawn the endless ages,
Why round his children here below
　The howling tempest rages;
But *this* we know, that life nor death
　Our souls from him can sever!
We'll praise him with our latest breath—
　We'll sing his praise forever!

WORDS OF CHEER FOR FAINTING CHRISTIANS.

Poor pilgrim, weary with the toils of life, distressed and afflicted on every hand, persecuted and forsaken by thy fellowmen, hast thou ever fathomed the depths of that glorious declaration, "I will never leave thee, nor forsake thee"?—Heb. 13:5. Hast thou ever realized that in whatever situation thou mayest be placed—on the mountains of delight or in the vale of humiliation, in sickness or in health, in prosperity or in adversity, in life or in death—thou art under the immediate protection of the great Shepherd of Israel, who never sleeps nor slumbers? The heavens may gather blackness, the storm may come down in fury, but He who whispered, "Peace, be still," to the raging billows, is "the same yesterday, to-day and forever"; and though now invisible his presence is with thee as truly and as really as it was with the timid band of disciples on the stormy sea of Galilee. The same Jesus that walked the streets of Jerusalem,— the pitiful, the affectionate, the tender-hearted,—is an eye-witness of all thy tears, thy trials and temptations. His ear, which was never closed to the cry of the poor and needy, is still open to thy call; and the heart which embraced the whole universe has a place for thee. The fires upon thy altar may have grown dim; the sacrifice may have been the poor and lean of thy flock; but the coals of divine love are bright upon the heavenly altar; and the great Sacrifice—the Lamb without spot or blemish—whispers of Calvary and Gethsemane, and mentions thee in his intercession.

Amazing love! love never to be fathomed. Angels who wait to do his bidding, seraphim and cherubim who behold his face in glory, can ye comprehend the height and depth, the length and breadth of the Saviour's love? Ah! angels, and seraphim, and cherubim still bend above the mercy-seat and "desire to look into" these things; but ages on ages of eternity may roll away and the love that bowed the heavens for sinful and degraded mortals shall still remain an unsounded deep! And this love is for thee—for *thee*, poor pilgrim. Plunge then deeply into this unfathable ocean. Fear not to loosen thy hold upon the shore: there is nothing there worthy thy love. Thou art an heir of immortality, and the pleasures which endure for a season should be nothing to thee.

Wealth, and honor, and power are only the gildings of a groaning and sin-cursed earth. The shouts of mirth and revelry borne upon the midnight air, are only the prelude to tears and sighs and mourning. Behind thee is the blackness of despair, before thee the everlasting sunshine. Away, away! tarry not to sip water from the broken cistern, for the living fountain gushes forth, clear as crystal; and the invitation is for all: "Ho, every one that thirsteth" (Isa. 55 : 1; Rev. 21 : 6; 22 : 17).—*Aug.* 10, 1856.

Miscellany.

THE DYING YEAR.

Hark! there comes at midnight hour
   Sound like funeral knell,
Chaining us with magic power,
   Whispering, "*Farewell.*"

'Tis the dying year's last sigh
   Mingling with the storm;
Closes now his hollow eye,
   Sinks his feeble form.

Still at midnight, dark and lone,
   Mournful echoes ring,
Murmuring in solemn tone,
   "*Time is on the wing.*"

INCOMPREHENSIBILITY OF GOD.

O God, where art thou? where thy mighty throne?
Why is thy face unseen, and thou unknown?—
Source and support of all, why is thy form
Hidden from mortal eyes? when every storm
That sweeps athwart the dark and angry sky,
When all the bright and burning orbs on high,
When the deep sea that in its fury roars,
When all its beautiful and fertile shores,
When every river, hill and lowly dale,
When every mountain, tree, and flowery vale,

When every bird, and e'en the springing sod,
Whisper aloud, " *There is, there is a God!* "

These are thy works ; but where, O God, art thou ?
Pavilioned in deep darkness, is thy brow
Hid in dark folds, ne'er to be drawn apart ?
Will mortal never see thee as thou art ?
Yes ; when the wheels of time have ceased to run,
When yon bright orb its glorious task has done,
Then will the veil be rent which once concealed
The throne of God, the mighty unrevealed ;
Then human eyes will view his dwelling-place,
And saints, as angels, see him face to face.

THE STAR OF BETHLEHEM.

Lo in the east the Star begins to rise,
The glorious centre for admiring eyes
Of men and angels—Herald of the morn
So long foretold, the Prince of peace is born !
O'er all the earth let hallelujahs ring,
Let all the earth a fitting tribute bring—
With gold and silver, frankincense and myrrh.
Come from the south, or, clad in robes of fur,
Come from the frozen north, from east and west,
Prince, priest and warrior, earth's great ones and best,
Come to the manger, humbly there lay down
The sword, the mitre and the jeweled crown.

The rich and noble celebrate the day
With pomp and show ; but who are these ? make way
Ye sons of wealth ! ye rulers stand aside !
This is no place, this is no hour for pride ;
The sick, the lame, the blind, the deaf, the dumb,
The sinful, poor and sorrowful may come ;

And even I can bring my little store—
A weary, sin-sick heart—I've nothing more:
The world may frown, the lofty may despise,
The gift is precious in my Saviour's eyes.
To him as sacred are the tears that fall
In lowly cottage as in princely hall,—
No rich, no poor his loving bosom knows,
He cares for all and pities all their woes,
In the same censer offers up their prayers,
And on his heart their names alike he bears.

O Star above all stars! whose blessed light
Illumes the darkness of our moral night,
Still guide our wandering feet till He whose birth
Thou didst announce shall come again to earth,
And wise and simple, king and subject meet
To hear their doom before the judgment-seat,—
Till nature's groans with human groans shall cease,
And Earth itself, once more with Heaven at peace,
Shall put her robes of deathless beauty on,
Time be no more, and the millennium dawn!

GOD MADE ME POOR.

God made me poor—am I to blame?
   And shall I bow my head
As though it were some dreadful shame
   I had inherited?

Shall I among the rich and great
   Like trembling culprit stand,
Or like obedient servant wait
   To do their least command?

And when they pass me by in scorn—
   As they have often done,—

Shall I regret that I was born
  An humble farmer's son?

No! should it ever cause a sigh
  This were indeed a shame;
For all unworthy then were I
  To bear my father's name.

I'll pay to all the homage due
  Whatever rank they hold;
But to my manhood ever true
  I will not bow to gold.

THE STRANGER GUEST.

Came a stranger, sad and weary,
  To my humble cot one day,
And he asked me for a shelter,—
  Long and rough had been the way
    He had traveled
  On that sultry summer day.

Pain and grief had marred his beauty,
  And a tear was in his eye
As he asked me for a shelter,
  And then waited a reply.
    Tears did gather
  In mine own, I knew not why.

'Neath my humble roof I led him,
  As he crossed the threshold o'er
"Peace to thee," he softly whispered;
  Peace I never knew before
    Filled my bosom,
  As the stranger filled my door.

Be my friend and guest forever,
 In a trembling voice I said;
And he smiled and laid so gently
 One dear hand upon my head;
  It was bleeding,
 And I knew for me it bled!

"I will be thy guest forever,"
 Said the stranger unto me;
"But the cost—say, hast thou counted—
 Counted what the cost will be?
  Earthly pleasures,
 Wilt thou leave them all for me?

"Wilt thou take my yoke upon thee?
 Wilt thou humbly bear my name?
Crush the risings of ambition,
 And the hopes of earthly fame?
  Freely suffering,
 For my sake, reproach and shame?"

Then I said, Both fame and pleasure
 Willingly I can resign;
Let me only feel thy presence,
 Let me know that thou art mine,
  And dear Saviour,
 All I have and am are thine!

A LONG DELIGHTFUL WALK.

While reading to-day an account of the descendants of Adam my mind was particularly struck with the short but comprehensive narrative of Enoch: "He walked with God, and he was not; for God took him"

(Gen. 5 : 21-24). He "walked with God," and how long? "Three hundred years" after he begat Methuselah. Oh, how strange that it should be so hard for me to walk in the commandments of the Lord even for a few days! O God, give me more of the love and more of the faith that Enoch possessed.—*Aug.* 18, 1853.

"THE SERVANT IS NOT ABOVE HIS MASTER."

Lonely pilgrim, art thou sinking
   'Neath the weight of grief and care?
Bitter dregs of sorrow drinking
   From the cup of dark despair?
Mourn not, for thy Master's footsteps
   The same gloomy paths have trod;
He has drained the cup of anguish,—
   He, the mighty Son of God.

Does gaunt poverty surround thee,
   With its pale and meagre train?
Do they gather closely round thee,
   Want, and suffering and pain?
Mourn not, for the chilly dew-drops
   Fell upon thy Master's bed;
Mourn not, for the Prince of Glory
   Had not where to lay his head!

Are thy kindred lowly lying
   In the cold and silent tomb,
Heedless of thy plaintive sighing,
   Heedless of thy grief and gloom?
Know thy Master's tears descended
   Where a dearly-loved one slept;

He knows well thy weight of sorrow;
    Murmur not, for Jesus wept.

Do the friends that once caressed thee
    Pass thee by with frowning brow?
Has the friendship that once blessed thee
    Changed to bitter hatred now?
Weep not, for thy Master's brethren
    In his sorrow turned aside,
Scorned to own that once they loved him;
    Weep not,—Jesus was denied!

Does a scoffing world deride thee,
    And expose to scorn and shame?
Do thy foes rise up beside thee,
    Blast thy character and name?
Know thy Master was derided,
    Scorned in Pilate's judgment-hall.
Mourn not; Christ, the great Redeemer,
    Was despised and loathed by all.

Art thou torn with grief and anguish?
    Racked with many a burning pain?
Does thy weary body languish?
    Fearful pangs torment thy brain?
Murmur not; from Calvary's mountain
    List thy Master's dying groan!
Murmur not; thy great Redeemer
    Gave his life to save thine own!

Does the monster Death look dreary?
    Fill thy mind with fears and gloom?
Does thy spirit, faint and weary,
    Shrink in terror from the tomb?
Know thy Master's gone before thee,
    Crossed the dark and narrow tide,

Disarmed Death of all his terrors :
   Then fear not—thy Saviour died!

Yes, he died,—the Prince of Glory,—
   Died upon the cursed tree ;
Pilgrim, spread the joyful story :
   Jesus died, and died for thee !
And he rose,—he rose triumphant,—
   Burst the bars of death in twain.
Lonely pilgrim, that same Jesus
   Will return to earth again !

See the first faint beams of morning
   Chasing night and clouds away,
All the glorious sky adorning ;
   Pilgrim, it is break of day !
Rouse thee, pilgrim, weep no longer ;
   Let thy glad Hosanna ring !
Jesus comes in power and glory ;
   Hail thy Saviour and thy King !

ELIJAH.

He calmly stands on the mountain's brow.
God shield thee, thou lonely prophet, now !
For thy friends are few, and thy foes are strong,
And each heart beats high in that mocking throng ;
And every eye is fixed upon thee,
As thou standest alone in thy majesty.

The prophets of Baal are many and great,
And they move along in princely state ;
With a scornful eye and a haughty air,
They have proudly taken their station there ;
While the blood of thy comrades stains the sod,
And thou only art left a prophet of God.

Yet firm is thy step, and calm thy brow—
The Lord God of hosts is for thee now;
And, strong in his strength, thou mayest advance,
And defy the world with thy piercing glance;
While the prophets of Baal bend at thy nod,
And the people own that the Lord, he is God.

The sun shines bright in the azure sky,
And the morning breeze sweeps gently by,
And all is quiet on earth, in air—
Not a sound escapes from that multitude there;
Though eager each eye and troubled each mien,
Yet the stillness of death reigns over the scene.

But a voice is heard; and clear and loud
It breaks on the ears of the listening crowd;
They quickly obey. A space is cleared;
The bullock is slain, the altar is reared;
While the prophets of Baal around it bend,
And implore their god an answer to send.

The day wears on, and the sun is high—
Still round that altar they madly cry;
But the sky is serene as ever before,
And, frantic with rage, they shout the more;
But 't is all in vain; and the day has past,
And the prophets of Baal have yielded at last.

Each heart beats high with anxiety there,
As Elijah, with calm, majestic air,
Alone and exposed to a nation's frown,
Rebuilds the altar long since thrown down.
'T is the hour for the evening sacrifice now,
And he solemnly kneels on the mountain's brow.

On the name of the Lord his God he calls;
When, lo! quick as lightning, the fire falls!

A smoke ascends to the vaulted sky,
And with it arises a mingled cry;
And bowed is each head, and bent is each knee
As "The Lord, he is God!" rings loud o'er the sea.

'T is night, and the evening breeze grows chill;
The prophet pleads with Jehovah still;
He has seen the prophets of Baal slain,
And now he implores for the falling rain.
The heavens grow black at Jehovah's word;
Arise, Elijah, thy prayer is heard!

THE SACRED PAGE.

Golden-headed youth and silver-headed age
Bend together earnestly o'er the Sacred Page;
One amid spring blossoms, while the falling leaves
Gather round the other sitting 'mid the sheaves;
One amid the twilight of the coming day,
While the shadows deepen round the other's way.

Golden-headed youth and silver-headed age
Read the same sweet lessons from the Sacred Page;
Eyes that brim with laughter, eyes that dim with years,
Resting there pay tribute in a flood of tears;
Rosy lips and pallid trembling at the cry—
Mournfully repeating the Sabachthani!

Golden-headed youth and silver-headed age
Draw their consolation from the Sacred Page;
One is in the valley where the grass is green,
While the other gazes on a wintry scene;
Both have lost their birth-right—both have felt their loss,
And they both regain it through the blessed Cross!

Golden-headed youth and silver-headed age,
Find their way to Heaven in the Sacred Page;
Like the little children waiting to be blessed,
One goes forth rejoicing to the Saviour's breast,
While the other clingeth to his mighty arm,
'Mid the swelling Jordan feeling no alarm.

Golden-headed youth and silver-headed age,
Come, and seek for treasures in the Sacred Page;
To the one how tender is the Saviour's call;
Yet the invitation He extends to all;
Earthly fountains fail you—hasten to assuage
Every grief of childhood—every pang of age!

Oh, what a book is the Bible! There is enough in one verse to condemn the whole world, and enough in another to redeem it.

No man in a dark night can behold himself in a mirror until a lamp is lighted,—and not even then distinctly and perfectly until the dawn of day: so no man can see himself in God's mirror until the beams of the divine lamp [the Holy Spirit] illume his soul,— nor even then can he see perfectly what a wretched and distorted being he is "until the day break" and, being made like his Saviour, he contrasts what he is with what he once was.

BEHOLD HOW HE LOVED US.

While on the cross the Saviour bleeds,
While friend nor foe his anguish heeds,
While many a taunt and bitter jeer
Break harshly on his holy ear,

He prays,—what can that last prayer be?
Oh, wondrous love, he prays for me!

Deep anguish fills his troubled soul,
The streams of blood in torrents roll;
And louder railings now are heard;
He breathes not one complaining word;
Yet, hark! he prays,—what can it be?
Oh, wondrous love, he *prays* for me!

He bows his head, Immanuel dies;
Darkness o'erspreads the azure skies,
Loud thunders shake the earth and air,
And earthquakes heave in horror there;
Angels the act with wonder see;
Oh, matchless love, he *dies* for me!

He leaves the dark and gloomy grave,
While angel-pinions round him wave,
And, rising from the mountain's brow,
Appears before his Father now;
He pleads,—what can those pleadings be?
Oh, deathless love, he *pleads* for me!

And can I then such scenes behold,
And still be careless, still be cold?
Can I, with air of sinful pride,
Cast such unbounded love aside?
My soul, oh, can it, *can it* be?
Has Jesus died in vain for thee?

Oh, no! the crimson streams that glide
From Calvary's deeply blood-stained side,
Invite my soul, so stained with sin,
To wash away its guilt therein;
And in those precious drops I see
Christ has not died in vain for me!

The Saviour pleads, in thrilling tone,
Before his mighty Father's throne,
That for his sake my guilty name
Within the book of life may claim
A place. He smiles; and now I see
Christ does not plead in vain for me!

Amazing love! what tongue can tell
The wondrous depths that in thee dwell?
What angel's mind can e'er explore
The riches of thy boundless store?
Oh, matchless love beyond degree,—
Christ bled, he died, and pleads for *me!*

LOVE YOUR ENEMIES.

Arrows dipped in poison flew
  From the fatal bow;
And they pierced my bosom through,
  And they laid me low.

Every nerve to anguish strung,
  In distress I cried:
And the waste around me rung,
  But no voice replied.

"Cruel was the hand," I said,
  "That could draw the bow:
Curses rest upon the head
  Of my heartless foe!"

Turning straightway at the sound,
  In the tangled wood,
Pale, and bearing many a wound,
  There a stranger stood.

Mournfully on me he gazed,
　Not a word he said:
But one hand the stranger raised,
　And I saw it bled.

Blood was flowing from his side
　And his thorn-pierced brow;
"Who has wounded thee?" I cried,
　And he answered, "*Thou!*"

Then I knew the Stranger well,
　And with sobs and tears
Prostrate at his feet I fell,
　But he soothed my fears.

"Thou hast wounded me, but live,—
　And my blessing take:
Henceforth wilt thou not forgive
　Freely for my sake?"

Resting in his fond embrace,
　Eased of every woe,—
Then I said, with smiling face,
　"Jesus, bless my foe!"

THE ORPHAN.

The storm was loud; a murky cloud
　O'erhung the midnight sky,
And rude the blast that wildly passed
　A lonely orphan by;
But ruder still the bitter thrill
　Of woe that rent his heart;
Darker his fears, sadder the tears
　That evermore would start.

"Bleak is the storm, and on my form
    The winds in fury beat;
A racking pain torments my brain,
    And sore these weary feet;
No ray of light illumes the night,
    And here, alas! I roam,
Where tempests howl and wild beasts growl;
    Oh, that I had a home!

"Full many a day has rolled away
    Since I have laid me down,
To cease to weep, and fall asleep,
    Save on the cold, damp ground;
And many more may pass me o'er
    Ere I may cease to roam;
One year ago it was not so,—
    For then I had a home!

"Then on his child a father smiled,
    And fondly me caressed;
When sorrow came, or bitter pain,
    I leaned upon his breast;
He'd kiss my cheek, and kindly speak
    In soft and soothing tone;
Oh, what a strange and dreary change—
    For then I had a home!

"When evening gray shut out the day,
    Beside my mother's knee,
With simple air I breathed the prayer
    That mother taught to me;
Then laid me down, not on the ground,
    Not on this cold, damp stone;
But on my bed, love made instead,—
    For then I had a home!

"The livelong day I spent in play
    Around our peaceful cot,
Or plucked the flowers from blooming bowers,
    And to my mother brought.
Then bliss and joy without alloy,
    And love around me shone;
Then hope could rest within my breast—
    For then I had a home!

"My father died, and by his side
    My darling mother sleeps;
And now their child in anguish wild
    Wanders around and weeps!
The pleasant cot my father bought
    A stranger calls his own;
With tearful face I left the place,
    For it was not my home!

"No home have I, no shelter nigh,
    And none my grief to share;
But I've a Friend, to him I'll bend,
    And he will grant my prayer.
He'll lend an ear for he can hear,
    Though high his mighty throne;
My steps he'll guide, and he'll provide
    The orphan with a home!

"Dark grows the sky, my lips are dry,
    And cold my aching brow;
Is this a dream?—for, lo! I seem
    To see my mother now!
Faint grows my breath, the arms of death
    Are surely round me thrown;
Oh, what a light breaks on my sight!
    There, there's the orphan's home!"

With smiling face in death's embrace
　　The orphan calmly slept;
He heard no more the tempest's roar;
　　No more the orphan wept.
No longer pain might rack his brain,
　　No longer might he roam,
The dearly loved he'd met above,
　　And found with them a home!

SENTENTIOUS PARAGRAPHS.

Rest, but few can comprehend the word. At morn I speak it, but at midnight most, and then 'tis music! Oh, the thought of *rest*—of perfect freedom from distress and pain—of health, of vigor in each nerve and limb. The thought inspires, consoles, and makes me pray for fear I shall lose the blessing. Grant me, O God, a patient heart; and may my will be so conformed to thine, that I may wait thy own good pleasure, whatsoever it be.

There are moments when Calvary overshadows Mount Sinai; when the blessed words, "It is finished," swell long and loud above the roar of thunder and the sound of trumpets; when the Cross conceals the Tables of stone bearing the holy law of the Almighty, and then I can boldly reply to the upbraidings of Conscience, "There is now no condemnation to them which are in Christ Jesus."

Sing, my heart, for the day cometh wherein the night shall be no more at all remembered; the clouds shall melt like vapor, and the voice of mourning and lamentation shall be heard no more forever. Awake and sing!

"YE DID IT NOT TO ME."

'Twas night—a dark and stormy night:
    The wintry winds were high;
Within the fire was blazing bright
And as I trimmed the cheerful light
    I heard a pleading cry.

"Come in," in hasty tones I said,
    The door flew open wide—
The tempest roared—I shrieked with dread,
For, lo, a Spectre from the dead
    Was standing by my side!

One icy hand was on mine own,
    I would have turned and fled:
But ah! my limbs were chilled to stone,
As in a low, sepulchral tone
    The sheeted Spectre said:

"It was a night like this I died,
    Scorned by my fellow men;
To me a shelter was denied
But when they slumber by my side,
    We shall be equals then.

"I starved—and thou wast clothed and fed,
    And had enough to spare;
Thou mightst have come with gentle tread,
And stood beside my dying bed,
    And found a blessing there.

"But now my curse : nor mine alone—
  The moment yet will be
When thou wilt stand before the Throne,
And hear it said in thunder tone :
  'Thou didst it not to Me.' "

The light grew dim throughout the room,
  Soon darkness reigned supreme,
But that pale Spectre from the tomb
Still eyed me through the dusky gloom,—
  Thank God, 'twas but a dream !

HEAR AND HELP ME.

Darkness and death are round me,
  The night is late ;
Yet once the Shepherd found me
  In such a state !
He lulled my fears to rest,
He took me to his breast ;
Is he less kind to-day ?
Lord Jesus, hear me pray !

Oh, hear me pray !
Remove the hateful sin
Which cankers all within
  And shrouds my way.
Oh, hear me in my anguish,
  My Saviour God !
I droop, I faint, I languish
  Beneath thy rod :
I tremble on the brink,
Support me or I sink :
Oh, hear me while I cry ;
Oh, save me or I die !

FAREWELL.

We stood upon the lonely shore
  And watched the bounding bark
Which far away the loved ones bore,
  On billows wild and dark;
And then there came a gloomy sound
Mournfully, mournfully stealing around—
  And the sound was this,
    As it rose and fell
  O'er the broad expanse,—
    "*Farewell! farewell!*"

We sought our home—once bright and fair,
  No word of hope we said,
For Sorrow entered with us there,
  With slow and silent tread;
And came a voice from every room
Mournfully, mournfully through the gloom;
  And the voice was this,
    As it sadly fell
  On our aching hearts,—
    "*Farewell, farewell!*"

The garden that at morn was gay,
  And the sequestered bower,
Seemed to have wept their bloom away,
  All in one little hour;
We heard a voice upon the breeze
Sigh mournfully, mournfully through the trees,
  And the voice was this,
    As it rose and fell
  On the balmy air,—
    "*Farewell, farewell!*"

Years, weary years have passed us o'er
  Since that unhappy morn,

And in our arms we clasp once more
  With rapture our first-born.
And thankful for our Father's care
Gratefully, gratefully raise the prayer,
  That when life is o'er
    Our anthems may swell
  Where lips breathe no more—
    Farewell, farewell!

NO MOTHER.

No mother! well, the burning tears may flow
  And bathe thy pillow, hapless orphan, now;
No mother's tender voice may soothe thy woe,
  No mother's kiss is on thy aching brow.

Thou hearest footsteps passing by the door,
  Oft hast thou heard thy mother's footsteps there;
But ah! she comes, unhappy boy, no more
  To say " Good night " or hear thy evening prayer.

Weep on: there's none to wipe away thy tears,
  There's none on earth thy mother's place to fill;
The night seems dark, but when the morn appears
  Darkness and gloom will be around thee still.

For thou hast lost what time can ne'er restore,
  What other friends, though kind, can never be;
She had bright visions of a better shore
  But asked to live—it was alone for thee.

Kneel, wretched orphan, kneel beside thy bed;
  Thy voice is choked, thy sobs have louder grown;
No mother's hand is lying on thy head,
  No mother's heart is lifted with thy own.

But thou canst pray, and on the Saviour's breast,
  Which feels for every grief and every care,
Pillow thy head and sweetly sink to rest,
  A *more than mother* will protect thee there.

TO A MOTHER ON THE DEATH OF HER CHILD.

Mother, thy loved one slumbers now
  In deep, unbroken rest;
But slumbers not with smiling brow
  Upon thy tender breast.
Oh, no! for Death with cruel dart,
  Unheeding anguish wild,
Has rudely torn thy yearning heart,
  And borne away thy child.

Thy home is drear at break of day,
  And drear at set of sun;
For, lo! the grave enwraps the clay
  Of thy departed one.
And vainly does thy spirit sigh,
  With yearnings deep and wild,
To clasp once more within thy arms
  Thy dear, thy darling child.

Cold Death has snatched thy lovely flower;
  But, lo! the day draws near,
When even Death shall lose his power,
  And thy sweet child appear
All glorious with immortal life,
  In Eden's garden fair.
Oh, mother, mother! would'st thou meet
  Thy dearly-loved one there?

Oh, would'st thou join the blood-washed throng
  On that immortal shore?

Oh, would'st thou swell the Conqueror's song
  And greet thy child once more ?
Then turn to Him who died for thee
  A death of woe and pain ;
And at the resurrection morn
  Embrace thy child again !

IN GOODNESS IS TRUE GREATNESS.

[The following lines were addressed to her brother on receiving a locket containing his daguerreotype.]

I touch the spring—and lo, a face
  Which for these many years
Within my heart has had a place,
  A tender place—appears.

The large dark eyes look up to mine,
  So like thyself!—the cheek,
The brow, the features, all are thine:
  Speak to me, brother, speak !

And tell me of each grief and care :
  For be they great or small,
A sister's heart would take a share—
  And, if it could, take all !

And tell me of each hopeful plan,
  And how the future seems,—
Oh, may that future to the man
  Be all the boy now dreams.

I've heard thee say thou wouldst be great,
  And with the gifted shine ;
'T is well ; but there's a nobler fate,
  I pray it may be thine :

It is to be an honest man,—
  To elevate thy race,
And like the good Samaritan
  Do good in every place;

To struggle bravely for the right,
  Though kings defend the wrong;
To live as in thy Maker's sight,
  And in his strength be strong;

To put the spotless garment on,
  To keep it pure and white,
And when the endless day shall dawn
  Receive a crown of light.

Dear brother, fame is but a breath,
  So I implore for thee
A holy life, a happy death,
  A blest eternity.

SIMILES.

Beneath the snow and frost of winter there are living seeds which shall produce abundant harvests: so beneath a cold exterior there may be a heart full of high resolves and glorious impulses, which at the right season shall burst into blossom and bear precious fruit.

How often the sun rises in a cloudless sky, to be obscured before noonday! Human life is like our fickle clime: to-day all sunshine, and to-morrow clouds.

The sun is the same by day and night, but the earth comes betwixt his light and us: so when the Sun of righteousness seems to have left our horizon and we turn in vain to the right and the left to find him, may it not be that the dark, dense earth has come betwixt us and his life-giving beams, while He remains "the same yesterday, to-day and forever"?

The thistle has a fragrant smell, and the thorn a pleasant fruit. It is a disease in the shell-fish that makes the pearl: so your sickness, my friend, may be the means of your winning the Pearl of great price.

What plant would thrive if the sun shone forever? and what should we be if the sun of prosperity always shone upon our pathway? Along life's dusty thoroughfare I see the world, but not as I saw it once: sickness and sorrow have given me another pair of eyes.

> Gentle breezes, balmy breezes,
>   There is vigor in your breath,
> But ye cannot bring the roses
>   To the leaden cheeks of death!

The soil that produces the rankest weeds would by proper care and cultivation produce the richest crops: so will the human heart when regenerated by grace and truth.

The violet cannot become the rose, the daisy cannot be the lily; and if they could all be the loveliest flower, earth would lose half its beauty. Without variety, a scene however fair within itself soon wearies us. Knowest thou the moral? Be content in thy proper sphere: thou mayest be the violet or the daisy, but envy not the rose and the lily; all are beautiful when in their appointed place.

At morn the shadows slant toward the west, but toward the east at night: so when the sun of life declines the shadows stretch away toward the everlasting hills whence the eternal beams of day shall arise.

THE CRUCIFIED OF GALILEE.

Methought I stood, at close of day,
Where soft the balmy breezes play,
And bright beneath the Eastern skies
The sacred hills of Canaan rise,
And saw him on the shameful tree,—
   The Crucified of Galilee!

I heard the mocking throng deride
The anguish of the Crucified;
I saw the brilliant sun grow dim;
I heard creation shriek for him;
I saw him die, and die for me,—
   The Crucified of Galilee!

And then I saw the veil upraised
From the eternal world, and gazed
Upon the scene in deep surprise;
One form alone could fix my eyes;
I knew him, yes, indeed 'twas he,—
   The Crucified of Galilee!

And though upon his lovely brow
A beam of glory rested now;

Though angels praised his holy name;
Yet still I knew he was the same
Who hung upon the shameful tree,—
  The Crucified of Galilee!

I knew him by his tender air;
I knew him by the fervent prayer
He breathed for those for whom he died;
I knew him by his wounded side;
By these I knew that it was he,—
  The Crucified of Galilee!

I knew him by the loving smile
With which he welcomed sinners vile;
I knew him, for he took a share
In all his children's griefs and care;
I knew him by his love for me,—
  The Crucified of Galilee!

The vision faded from afar;
But still 't is memory's guiding star,
To cheer the night and point a way
Unto an everlasting day,
When I, with unveiled eyes, shall see
  The Crucified of Galilee!

THE ASCENSION.

A well-known group stood on the mountain side
And in their midst appeared the Crucified.
Oft had they stood in that sequestered place,
Their beaming eyes fixed on their Saviour's face;
But never met on Olivet's fair brow
With such emotions as they cherished now;
And never with such eager spirits hung

Upon the words that fell from Jesus' tongue;
For never had their Master's voice before
Sounded so sweet as when—his mission o'er,—
He gathered round him that devoted band,
To give his blessing and his last command:
"Go ye, and teach all nations in my name—
The Jew and Greek, the bond and free, the same;
But first proclaim a Saviour's love to those
Who thirsted for his blood, and mocked his woes,
That they, believing, through his death may live,
And know their risen Saviour can forgive.
Ye shall declare salvation's waters free,
And bid all nations to the fountain flee;
And though ye meet with perils dark and drear,
And tribulation be your portion here,—
Though persecution, with uplifted sword,
Shall call for blood, and your own blood be poured,—
Yet know that I, your Saviour and your friend,
Will be with you till life itself shall end;
And with all those who boldly shall proclaim
To a lost world salvation through my name,
In every land, in every age and clime,
Till the last trump shall sound the knell of time."

·   ·   ·   ·   ·   ·   ·   ·   ·   ·

The humble followers of the Nazarene
In silent awe gazed on the wondrous scene;
Beheld their Lord in power and glory rise
Up the bright pathway of the parting skies;
And while they strove with piercing eyes in vain
To catch one glimpse of that dear form again,
Two angels left the bright and heavenly shore,
And messages of joy and love they bore.
Oh, glorious message to that faithful band,
Who on the mountain's top bewildered stand!
Oh, glorious sound to every ransomed soul,

From sea to sea, from spreading pole to pole
In every age, oh, tell the tidings o'er—
"That very Jesus shall return once more!"
Hark! angel-voices rend the vaulted sky,
In thrilling tones those shining angels cry,
"Why stand ye gazing on yon glistening dome?
Heaven has received your risen Master home!
The time will come, when, as ye saw him rise,
He shall descend in power the parted skies."

THE HEBREW'S LAMENT.

Thou art the land of all my dreams,—
    Thy wanderer's heart is thine,
And oft he lingers by thy streams,
    O holy Palestine!

A stranger in a stranger's land
    O'er hill and vale I roam;
But hope forever points her hand
    Towards my father's home.

They tell me that on Zion's hill
    The Cross and Crescent shine:
But oh, my heart is with thee still,
    Beloved Palestine.

I know that Israel's weary race
    Are scorned on every shore,
And scarcely find a dwelling-place
    Where they were lords before.

Yet, 'mid the darkness and the gloom,
    A light begins to break;
O Israel, from the dreary tomb
    Thy buried hopes awake,—

And lips that raise the fervent prayer,
  "How long, O Lord, how long?"
Shall change the wailings of despair
  To the triumphant song.

And I may live to see the hour—
  The hour that must be near,—
When in his royalty and power
  Our Shiloh will appear.

Till then my prayers will rise for thee,
  Till then my heart be thine,
O land beyond the stormy sea,
  O holy Palestine.

WHEN SHALL I RECEIVE MY DIPLOMA?

For many long years I have been in the school of affliction, and during that time how often I have asked the questions, When will my course be completed? when shall I receive my diploma? But let me first consider: Am I prepared for the grand examination in which angels are to be the spectators, and God himself judge? Here teachers and professors—however skilled in human wisdom, friends and relatives—however anxious for my welfare, must step aside and leave me alone before the dread tribunal! In the presence of my fellow-creatures I might wear the robes of hypocrisy and appear in reality what I am not; but what would this avail me in the presence of Him who knows every thought even before it is formed, and whose searching eye can take in at a single glance the past, present, and future of my history?

O dreaded hour! who can wonder that timid mortals put it far in the distance, and even strive to shut their eyes to its stern reality? What folly! Were the light of revelation quenched forever, there is that within every human breast which warns of a judgment to come and of a righteous retribution. Swift as the planets roll in their orbits around the sun, still swifter advances that terrible scene around which the hopes and fears, the joys and miseries of eternity cluster. It is the great centre of attraction, not only for one age or one nation, but for all who have drawn the breath of life from the grand creation anthem of stars and angels (Job 38 : 4–7) till stars and angels again lift up their voices in concert, and swear that "Time shall be no longer." Yet the life, the heart of each individual there will be as closely examined as if the court of Heaven were sitting for him alone, and he the only person for whom the joys of Paradise or the pains of Hell were prepared by eternal Justice!

ALONE WITH JESUS.

Alone with Jesus! leave me here,
Without a wish, without a fear,—
My pulse is weak and faint my breath
But is He not the Lord of death?
And if I live, or if I die,
'T is all the same when He is nigh.

Alone with Jesus! ye who weep,
And round my bed your vigils keep,
My love was never half so strong,
And yours—oh, I have proved it long,
But when had earthly friend the power
To comfort in a dying hour!

Alone with Jesus! oh, how sweet
In health to worship at his feet!
But sweeter far when day by day
We droop, and pine, and waste away,
To feel his arms around us close,
And in his bosom find repose!

Alone with Jesus! how secure,
Vile in myself, in him how pure;
The tempests howl, the waters beat,
They harm me not in my retreat;
Night deepens—'mid its gloom and chill
He draws me nearer to him still.

Alone with Jesus! what alarms
The infant in its mother's arms?
Before me death and judgment rise,—
I turn my head and close mine eyes,
There's naught for me to fear or do,
I *know* that he will bear me through!

Alone with Jesus! earth grows dim,—
I even see my friends through him;
Time, space, all things below, above,
Reveal to me one Life, one Love,—
That One in whom all glories shine,
All beauties meet—that One is mine!

THE LOST BABE.

There was a bower that love had reared
    And beautified with care ;
One day a messenger appeared
    And asked admission there.

He was not welcome to the bower,
    For something in his face,
Where'er he went, had always power
    To cloud the brightest place.

Love barred the door, and cried, "Forbear,
    Thou art no bidden guest";
Then gathered up her jewels rare
    And hid them in her breast.

Still louder knocked he than before,
    And still he was denied;
Then, laughing at the well-barred door,
    He threw it open wide.

"I come from Paradise above,"
    The messenger began:
"Oh, not in anger but in love
    God worketh out his plan.

"Sent from the King's eternal throne
    My mission to fulfill,
I ask one jewel of thine own,—
    It is the Master's will :

"One birdling from the parent nest,
    One lamb from out thy fold,
To nestle in the Saviour's breast
    As did the babes of old.

"How safe! Her resting-place how sweet!
　　But thou wilt sadly miss
　The busy hands, the dancing feet,
　　The prattle and the kiss.

"There comes an hour, so long foretold
　　That many deem it vain,
　When in his arms thou shalt behold
　　That precious lamb again.

"When earth and sea at God's command
　　Their treasures shall restore
　Then thou shalt clasp this little hand,
　　Nor dread a parting more."

Love wept—her very bosom bled
　　For that lost little one;
But Faith supported her and said,
　　"The Master's will be done."

THE DAY OF WRATH.

"*The great day of his wrath is come; and who shall be able to stand?*"
—Rev. 6 : 17.

The nations tremble, and the isles are moved;
　All cheeks are gathering paleness; lips are dumb
That smiled in scorn but yesterday, or proved
　The day of wrath would not for ages come;
Each eye is fixed—there seems nor life nor breath
In that vast human sea,—but ah! it is not death.

The morning broke in splendor, as it rose
　Upon the fated Cities of the Plain;
And men went forth refreshed from their repose,
　Where duty called them, or the love of gain;

When sudden as the lightning's vivid glare
Like heated furnace glowed the earth, the sea, the air.

From the Equator to the frozen Pole,
   All nations saw, and understood " the sign ";
The seventh angel sounded ! like a scroll
   The heavens departed, and a Form divine
And awful in its grandeur was revealed,—
The sun and moon grew pale, and earth astounded reeled.

Then rose a wail of anguish and despair—
   By men, by angels, never heard before ;
The tones of earth and hell were mingled there,
   Henceforth to be thus mingled evermore
Beyond the reach of Mercy's loving ear,
Who wept and pleaded once—but will no longer hear.

But hark ! in contrast what a shout of joy
   Goes up to heaven ; it tells of victory won
O'er sin and death, o'er all that can destroy,—
   It tells of life eternal just begun,—
Of bliss coeval with the endless years,—
Of love that waited long for Him who now appears.

My soul consider—'t is no idle flight
   Of fancy, when she pictures thus the day
When sun and planets shall withdraw their light,
   And heaven and earth like smoke shall pass away ;
God hath declared it, and our Saviour hath,
And lo, it hastens fast—that dreadful day of wrath.

Where wilt thou find a shelter from the storm ?
   Not wealth, nor power, nor friends can succor then ;
How wilt thou gaze upon that glorious Form
   That seals the doom of angels and of men ?

How wilt thou stand before the judgment seat
And every idle word, and thought, and action meet?

O Lamb of God whose blood was shed for me,—
　Redeemer, Saviour, Lover of mankind,—
Spread over me thy robes, that I in Thee
　A shelter from that dreadful storm may find,—
And calm amid the tumult and despair
Look at the great white throne, and see my Surety
　　there!

THE BELIEVER'S SAFETY.

Ah, Christian, why is thy heart sad and thy brow clouded? Hast thou been gazing down into the depths of thine own soul, and art thou startled at what thou hast there seen? Hast thou met with evil thoughts which thou wouldst gladly never have harbored, and art thou despairing because of thy short-comings and unworthiness? Art thou looking to the future with dread, and trembling lest in the hour of trial and temptation thou wilt fall?

Turn away thine eyes from the pollution of thine own sinful heart, and gaze upon One who has become a perfect sin-offering for thee. True, thou art frail and unworthy, but the Lamb that was slain *is worthy*, and his perfection is enough for thee; his righteousness alone recommends thee to the Father. Dost thou trust in him with all thy heart? Dost thou hope for eternal life because he died? Then thou art safe. "The eternal God is thy refuge, and underneath thee are the everlasting arms." The storms may howl, and tempests may gather around thee; the billows may rage, but they only lash the Rock upon which thou standest. "Though the earth be removed, and the mountains be cast into the midst of the sea," yet thou art safe, for he who made the heavens and the earth is thy Father. He who commandeth the sun, and it riseth not, and sealeth up the stars; "who alone spreadeth out the heavens and treadeth upon the waves of the sea," is thy nearest and dearest friend. The same voice which said, "Let there be light, and there was light;" which commanded the raging waters, "Hitherto shalt thou come, but no farther: and here shall thy proud waves be stayed," is still whispering in thine ear, "Fear thee not, for I am with thee; be not dismayed, for I am thy God." Yes, thou art safe! thou art trusting in the mighty One of Israel, and thou shalt never be confounded.

Thou hast been looking away into the regions of the blessed; thou hast beheld with an eye of faith the things which God has prepared for those that love him, and amid the ineffable glory of that beautiful world thou hast heard the voices of the redeemed from the earth, saying: "Salvation to our God which sitteth upon the throne, and unto the Lamb," until thou hast longed to join with them in the song of redemption, singing praises forever and ever to him who has ransomed thee with his own precious blood. Then a cloud has gathered over thee, thy sinfulness has risen like a mountain, and thou hast sighed in thy spirit, "Oh, that I were sure of a part with them; oh, that I was safe as they!" and thou art as safe this moment with thy feet upon the Rock of Ages, as if thou didst walk the golden streets of the New Jerusalem, or bow with the angelic hosts around the dazzling throne of thy Creator. Thou art safe, for thy "life is hid with Christ in God"; and could'st thou ask for a surer hiding-place! Thou hast entered into an everlasting covenant with the King of kings, and while thou dost cling to his side shall it ever be broken? Thou hast entrusted thy soul into his hands, and is he not able to "keep that which thou hast committed unto him?" Thine enemies are many and powerful, but what are they compared to the living God? In the hour of temptation "he will never leave thee nor forsake thee"; when thy foes surround thee on every side, and the darkness of midnight gathers over thy soul, the Almighty arm shall lift up a standard, and thou shalt safely repose "under the shadow of his wings." "The Lord is thy rock, and thy fortress, and thy deliverer." "The Lord is thy light and thy salvation; whom shalt thou fear? The Lord is the strength of thy life, of whom shalt thou be afraid?"

Then look up, Christian! 'tis no time for desponding. The glittering spires of the Eternal City are already heaving in sight; perchance another storm, another beating against the fragile bark, and thou art there! Already the music of that glorious land steals softly over the roaring billows, and reminds thee thou art nearing the peaceful shore. Already the dark cloud which gathers above thy head is tinged with the beams of immortal glory, and away in the distance thou canst behold the first faint glimmerings of the Morning Star. Joy for thee, O wanderer! the shadows of the night are passing away, and the unclouded morning comes on apace!

<blockquote>
Yes, thou art safe! lift up thine eyes,
And calm thy anxious fears;
The Sun of glory gilds the skies,
And Christ thy life appears.
</blockquote>

www.ingramcontent.com/pod-product-compliance
Lightning Source LLC
Chambersburg PA
CBHW020924230426
43666CB00008B/1563